The Bible of Dark Psychology

The Only Book You'll Ever Need to Understand People's Thoughts, Actions, and How to Change Them.

HALBERT WARD

TABLE OF CONTENTS

INTRODUCTION

Have you been wondering how to get your way with your colleagues at work, bosses, prospects, and other important people present in your life so that you can manipulate them to get your desires and progress faster in life?

Do you want to learn and implement the tactics some individuals use to get what they want from people so that you can be able to spot any attempts by other individuals to do the same to you and use it to your advantage?

If your answer is yes, read on.

You are about to learn how to use the power of dark psychology to understand people's thoughts and actions and change them to your advantage.

Persuasion has fundamental principles. What can you do to make people say yes? How do clever marketing people, sleek salespeople, and sneaky confidence tricksters manipulate people? We will take a look at the psychology behind the techniques these people use, thereby opening your eyes to the tactics of manipulation and helping you unleash the persuasive powers you have within you.

When the word "manipulation" is used, there is usually a negative connotation to it. This is the case because no individual wants others to manipulate them into doing something. Manipulation and dark psychology are used by many individuals and companies to influence lives every day whether you like it or not. So, if you have been trying to get people to do things for you and it's not working, would you like to learn more about these techniques? There may be many resources out there that may have left you confused, but this book will teach you how to use psychological manipulation.

Dark psychology is the phenomenon by which individuals use tactics of manipulation, persuasion, motivation, and coercion to achieve their desires. The tactics of dark psychology can be used for good or bad intentions, it all depends on the individual using it.

Wondering why people use psychological manipulation? People use it for a number of things. Numerous non-profits and charities use it for good. They use it to change the perspectives that people have, thereby helping them make positive changes in the world. Company managers also use psychological manipulation to influence their workers. Now imagine yourself equipped with the same knowledge about psychological manipulation that these individuals and organizations have and using it to influence people around you. Sounds good, right? This book will not only equip you with this knowledge but will also help you identify any negative manipulators present in your life.

This book introduces you to dark psychology and shows you how you can identify and protect yourself from it. It describes how you can use the skill effectively while interacting with other individuals. It explores ways individuals can control the minds of others around them through the use of simple techniques. You will be able to think more clearly and have a better mindset. It will then translate to a higher level of achievement in your goals. You will also learn how to influence other individuals to assist you in achieving your goals.

This book will help you in your personal and professional life. Emotional intelligence is important in life. You need it for your work and relationships. This book shows you ways in which to understand your emotions as well as the emotions of the people around you. When you have high emotional intelligence, you will be open to positive persuasion and be able to make other individuals feel good about themselves. Understanding your emotions will also help you learn how to become motivated and disciplined to achieve your goals.

You will learn more about body language and manipulation. When you master how to read the body language of people, you will be able to use it to your advantage. Whether it is your personal relationship or your workplace, you can use manipulation strategies to accomplish your goals. Mastering these manipulation techniques will help you in different situations in your life.

This book is an excellent guide to understanding people's thoughts and actions and how to change them using dark psychology. Manipulation differs from persuasion. You will learn how to protect yourself from manipulators and use the tactics to your advantage. When you can quickly read the body language of people, you will easily identify the positive influencers as well as the deceptive manipulators. You will learn how to influence people around you with your body language and words.

You need to understand the power of influence when it comes to changing the behavior of individuals and getting them to do what you want them to do. Understanding how individuals think will make you know how to easily get them to do what you want.

Once you master the skill of dark psychology, you will have the ability to convince people to do whatever you want them to do whenever you want them to do it. Also, you will learn how to protect your mind from other individuals, so manipulators that have evil intent can't manipulate you into doing whatever they want you to do.

People use dark psychology every day to get what they want. Corporations, politicians, and public speakers use it to get what they want from people. They use it to get votes, compliance, results, and purchases.

Body language and emotional intelligence play important roles in manipulation. Mastering these concepts will help you better gauge the individuals around you and understand what affects their actions and decisions. Understand that manipulation is not only used negatively. It is also used to make positive changes in the lives of the people around you and in your life as well.

Dark psychology, persuasion, and manipulation are inseparable from the business world, but are you aware that you can use these skills to reconcile with people or land yourself a job, a boyfriend, a girlfriend, and even achieve your goals?

If you are reading this book, it means you know how important it is to master the art of making people do what you want. Making people do what you want whenever you want them to do it is a skill you will need in life, especially if you are a businessman or woman. So, how can you make people do what you want them to do when you want them to do it? The solution to this is that you need to be able to read their minds and manipulate them.

The word manipulation has been tagged as something negatively inclined. But on the contrary, it can be used positively. Manipulation is when you make individuals do what you want whether they are doing it willingly or unwillingly. People do not usually wake up in the morning, to browse the internet hoping to purchase something. But the truth is, many people actually end up buying things they never intended to believe in the first place.

When you solve a problem for your audience, you are simply manipulating your audience to achieve your own goal by solving their problem. Your audience gets the solution to their problem, and you make your profit.

Studies show that a large percentage of job seekers also use dark psychology during the interview stage to land their jobs. Job seekers don't mention how often they were caught dozing off at work, and they never say how often they went to their previous workplace late. They usually don't disclose during interviews the main reason they were sacked from the job they were previously doing. Don't people often do this? Manipulating interviewers into seeing them as the perfect candidates for the job is something many job seekers do. But job seekers, influencers, advertisers, and many others do not call themselves manipulators, do they? And it's not surprising that they don't. Although manipulation alters people's views, behaviors, and even goals, you can use the techniques of dark psychology to further your interests.

Dark psychology is commonly used today. This book gives you an excellent introduction to the world of dark psychology and manipulation. You will discover that these tactics are used more often than you are aware of. Mastering these techniques will give you an advantage in both your personal as well as your professional life.

CHAPTER ONE:
Understanding Dark Psychology

Dark psychology can be used for good and evil purposes. It is capable of revealing much about the nature of humans and is used to describe the study of the human mind's dark characteristics. It is a study of how individuals use persuasion and manipulation to achieve their goals. Once an individual knows how to use dark psychology, it can be a powerful tool.

Dark psychology involves discovering the human mind's weaknesses and exploiting them. Practitioners of dark psychology understand how individuals think and feel and are able to manipulate individuals to do what they want them to do. Every human has the potential to victimize other people. While many control themselves and restrain this tendency, some others don't do that and end up acting upon their impulses.

Dark psychology involves coercion, deception, persuasion, and other strategies to influence people's emotions, thoughts, and behaviors without their awareness or consent. It is often related to criminal activities such as scams, fraud, terrorism, and abuse, but it can be used in everyday situations such as work, relationships, and politics.

Dark Psychology has been in existence since ancient times when individuals used superstition, suggestion, and hypnosis to control others. In the twentieth century, more sophisticated techniques have been developed for influencing and manipulating people as a result of the study of psychology. Dark Psychology has become more prevalent as a result of propaganda, advertising, and social media. Individuals, organizations, and groups can use these tactics, which range from subtle manipulation to overt coercion, to achieve their goals. When the wrong person uses dark psychology, it can be harmful and have serious consequences for both the individual being manipulated and the manipulator. Dark psychology includes every type of behavior, from self-destructive behaviors and manipulation to serial killers and criminals. People use this technique for a variety of reasons. Some individuals use it to achieve nefarious ends, and some others use it for more beneficial purposes. For example, therapists can help patients overcome their anxieties and fears by using techniques of dark psychology. Also, police officers may obtain convictions for criminals by using techniques of dark psychology.

Individuals in positions of authority often manipulate people around them through the use of manipulation and dark psychology techniques. For example, a politician with a troubled image could use techniques of dark psychology to influence the media to present spotless images of them to the public.

A salesman or woman can convince people to buy products they don't need by using manipulative tactics. A boss could control his employees and make them do what he wants them to do by using psychological tricks. These are examples of different individuals who might employ dark psychology tactics, but you need to remember that these tactics could be used on anyone.

Dark psychology techniques are used in society and culture to manipulate media coverage, influence public opinion, and shape political outcomes. Techniques such as misinformation, fake news, and propaganda are used to manipulate the attitudes and beliefs of individuals. The techniques can lead to conflict, division, and increased polarization. They are also capable of eroding democratic values and undermining trust in institutions. Examples of dark psychology include the spread of fake news during the time of elections, as well as the use of psychological techniques in marketing and advertising.

While manipulation and dark psychology may be considered illegal, some professions use these tactics to their advantage. For example, law enforcement officers often collect information on criminals through dark psychology. Also, dark psychology is used to study how the human mind works and to help people overcome challenges.

There are benefits you can get from understanding more about dark psychology and how to use it. Once you know how it works, you will be able to use it correctly when you find yourself in a situation that requires you to employ the strategies.

Dark psychology uses psychological principles in ways that benefit the wrongdoer and harm individuals. It involves coercion, control, manipulation, and, often, restricting the power and freedom of the individual on the receiving end. Psychological strategies are used to achieve one's desires at the expense of other people. Certain dark psychology tactics can be used to convince, persuade, and influence other people's thought patterns and minds, but the tactics won't work for every individual. Dark psychology works within the boundaries of logic and is not a sort of sorcery.

A key goal of dark psychology is to use social manipulation for social situations. Its goal is to benefit the dark psychologist regardless of how hurtful it is to the victims of the dark psychologist. Dark psychology involves influencing an individual's ideas without resorting to force or natural persuasive methods by using a set of characteristics.

Operant training is used to hack an individual's psyche and make them interested in the idea or information that is being presented to them. This means that the individual's behavior changes as a result of external causes. Mental conditioning and repetition affect a sensitive individual's way of processing information. This means that it will be possible for the same manipulator to manipulate them in the future.

In this book, we will delve deeper into dark psychology and its techniques. We will also discuss how it is applied in various contexts. It involves the art of manipulating and influencing people to serve the interests of the manipulator. It is important to emphasize that these techniques are about psychological manipulation but not about mind control. To better understand dark psychology and its techniques, you need first to understand your emotions and the emotions of others. The subsequent chapter will teach you this.

CHAPTER TWO:
Understanding Emotions

Do you enjoy connecting with people? The ability to identify emotions and understand both your emotions and other people's emotions is referred to as emotional intelligence. Studies have shown that emotional intelligence is a valuable and rare asset that can help you develop relationships, improve job satisfaction, and defuse conflict.

Emotions can impact our thoughts and behavior. Your daily emotions have the ability to influence both the small and big decisions you make about your life and can compel you to take action. Emotions can last long, such as sadness resulting from the end of a relationship, and they can be short-lived, for example, when you are briefly annoyed at a colleague at work. But what causes us to experience emotions? What role do emotions play in our lives? Where do they originate from?

We need to understand emotion's three components to understand emotions truly. Each of the elements can play a role in the purpose and function of your emotional responses. They include the subjective component, the physiological component, and the expressive component. The subjective component has to do with how a person experiences the emotion, the physiological component has to do with how the person's body reacts to the emotion, and the expressive component involves the person's actions in response to the emotion.

Emotions do the following:

Emotions keep you from danger
Emotions allow both humans and other animals to reproduce and survive. It is important for safety and survival. Your emotions will

tell you when danger is on the way, making you avoid it. Emotions can also get you ready to take action. The amygdala is what triggers the emotional responses that make your body get ready to handle things like anger and fear. This can trigger the body's fight-or-flight response and this results in physiological responses that make the body ready to flee to safety or stay back and face the danger. Emotions play a major role by causing you to quickly take action to increase your chances of success and survival.

Emotions help people understand how you are feeling

When you are having interactions with people, you need to help them understand how you are feeling. You can give clues that involve emotional expression where you use body language like different facial expressions that reflect the emotions you are experiencing. Sometimes, you might also need to directly state how you feel for people to understand your feelings.

When you tell your family members or friends that you are feeling frightened, sad, happy, or excited, you provide them with important information to help them take action. Studies show that individuals experience positive emotions more frequently than they experience negative emotions.

Emotions can be a source of motivation. When you have to write a difficult exam, it might get you so worried to the point that you are afraid you will not write it well and the results will negatively affect your final grade in school. The emotional responses might increase your likelihood of studying hard. When you experience a specific emotion, you can be motivated to do something that will help you get a good grade. To reduce the chances of facing negative emotions and enhance the likelihood of experiencing positive emotions, you tend to engage in specific actions. For instance, look for hobbies or activities that give you a sense of excitement, contentment, and happiness. And you would probably stay away from situations that might bore you, make you sad, or give you anxiety. Emotions make you more likely to take action. Anger can make you confront the source of an issue. Experiencing fear can make you flee a threat, and feelings of love can make you seek out a partner.

Emotions help you understand how others are feeling

In the same way that your emotions provide valuable information to other people, a wealth of social information is also given by the emotional expressions of the people around you. Social communication cannot be neglected in your relationships and daily life. It is an important part of life, and having the ability to react to other people's emotions and being able to interpret them is important.

It allows you to respond appropriately and develop more meaningful and deeper relationships with your family members, loved ones, and friends. It also gives you the opportunity to communicate effectively in different social situations, from managing an employee who is hot-headed to handling an angry customer.

Understanding other people's emotional displays helps us clearly understand the best response we can give in a particular situation.

Emotions have a major influence on your decisions

Your emotions can have an impact on the decisions you make, from which political candidates you decide to vote for during elections to what you choose to have for lunch. Studies have also shown that a reduced ability to make good decisions is experienced by individuals who have certain brain damage types that affect their ability to experience emotions.

Even in cases where you believe that rationality and pure logic guide your decisions, emotions play a major role. Emotional intelligence, which is your ability to understand your emotions and manage them, plays a key role in decision-making. Studies have shown that feeling anger or joy makes people quickly take action, feeling disgusted causes individuals to become more likely to do away with their belongings. Fear is capable of increasing perceptions of risk.

Strategies for Changing Someone's Mind

Have you ever engaged in a heated argument that initially started as a result of an attempt at a civil discussion about a situation, but led to insults? Many people have found themselves in such situations. Though you might have the feeling of satisfaction in the moment when you hurl derogatory insults at someone, it will never help them see things from your point of view. It is important to focus on compassion and curiosity and to be clear that you don't look down on the person you are talking to or think the person is the enemy.

More happiness and collaboration are possible if people can learn to communicate better with each other. It is important to approach conversations that we consider hard more effectively. Learning how to have a good conversation when different points of view arise is vital. The attempt can be made more effective by some strategies.

You can use these research-backed strategies actually to change a person's mind:

Practice listening with empathy

No matter what the person you are having a conversation with says, it's important to listen with empathy and non-judgmentally.

Suppose you tell the person that they are gullible, stupid, or should be ashamed. In that case, it will cause problems and ruin the possibility of having a conversation that would actually make the person reevaluate the matter or change their mind.

Studies show that empathizing with the individuals you disagree with may increase your political arguments' persuasiveness. When you use terms such as, I understand, we all want, and I agree with you, it can show empathy. If you see that you are running low on empathy, you can get it back up by first picturing the individual you are having a conversation with when they were a little child. Then think about some dream the person has that you support or one positive moment you have experienced with the individual.

17

Stay calm and open to learning

You need to enter a conversation with the right mindset. This entails striving to stay calm and willing to learn. If you know that you might snap since you are fired up, leave the issue and revisit it at another time.

Disclose any vulnerability or nervousness to the person you are having a conversation with. We often tend to want to hide our vulnerabilities or nervousness, but owning up to it can be helpful as it helps to soften people.

Avoid assuming that the individual you are talking to doesn't like you, even if you don't have the same views as them. If you begin a conversation with someone thinking that they don't want to listen to you and they hate your guts, the conversation will not go smoothly. Studies show that one powerful way to reduce partisan animosity is to correct that single misconception that the other person doesn't hate you as much as you initially thought.

The following exercises can help you open up your heart and create the right environment for a hard conversation:

Don't just use facts, but tell stories

Talking to a person and only firing facts at them is not often very effective. You need to share narratives and personal experiences as they will be more likely to understand what you are saying and it will be more effective.

When you connect on a human level and share your experiences, the effectiveness is higher than when you are simply arguing. People usually think that they need to argue aggressively to get their point across, but that is often ineffective.

A person can easily refute facts, but it is more difficult to refute experiences. That is why asking questions about an individual's personal experiences can be helpful. This is more helpful than their beliefs that shape their point of view, and you should avoid attacking them. It is possible if you are talking to a person who doesn't like to vote, and you are trying to change their mind about it. The person might be arguing that politicians never listen. Instead of directly telling them that they are wrong, you can share a story from your life about a time when you also felt like politicians didn't listen to what you said. This will help to form a connection with your conversation partner as they will feel like you are on their side. You can then share another story with them and talk about an experience that showed you that politicians actually listen, and how you got to know that they do. When you share stories during conversations, it encourages your conversation partner to open up and builds trust, while widening perspectives.

Look for a common ground

If you are attempting to change the mind of someone, you can't make the conversation in such a way that you keep correcting them. You have to connect with the person. You can start the conversation by looking for something that you and the person agree on.

If someone says that people need to stop the protests against police, for instance, you could agree with the person that there are definitely good police officers. This strategy entails that you agree to the point that you can with something their statement contains, even if you don't agree with the entire statement. You need to agree with them before challenging them. This strategy can make people keep an open mindset even before you say the new things you want to invite them to agree about.

Keep the door open to introspection

Many individuals have strong feelings about divisive issues but they never take the time to catalog the particular reasons why. You can create space for this individual actually to form their first opinion on the issue.

For instance, you might begin by asking a person a question using a scale of 1 to 10, about how strongly they feel about a particular topic. If the individual responds with a 6. You can ask them, "Why not a 5 or a 10?" When you ask that follow-up question, they will often pause and give you a well-articulated response. The individual you are having a conversation with might discover that they don't have opinions that are as strong as they had initially thought, and that room still exists for flexibility.

You can create a space where you say to the person, "I think you are a reasonable and rational person. I think we share similar views on a lot of the world's problems. I'm wondering why we do not agree on this particular issue, and I am seeking your permission to perform further investigation on the issue together."

Know when to step away

There are some conversations that will turn into arguments. If the individual you are having a conversation with insults you, you can switch things up and tell them you wanted to go back to something before they said something else, and then you can rewind the conversation you were having. It is fine to step away if things start to get out of hand. Take a break from the conversation. You can come up with an excuse of going to the restroom, and take some time to compose yourself before making up your mind whether or not to continue the conversation and how to continue it.

Set boundaries if you are online

You will find many annoying and long-winded posts and comments on social media. Productive and non-productive conversations alike happen there. People are usually anonymous online and you can't see their faces, so it is not hard to misconstrue their intentions and words.

You need to learn how to communicate more persuasively and productively, and online platforms can be one of the most fruitful places to do this.

You can do the following:

Politely set boundaries

Frame the request in a polite manner. You can say, "I want us to have this conversation, but it can't go smoothly if you question my motives or call me names. Can we come to an agreement to try to understand each other's perspective and treat each other with respect?" When you talk like this, it works most of the time.

Be human

Users of social media often forget that the people they are talking to on social media are real people, not robots that do not have feelings. When joining a conversation on social media, it's polite to introduce yourself and express pleasure in meeting others. This will help to change their orientation and put them into a different script.

Stay detached from the outcome

Have you ever watched someone trying to catch a butterfly in their hands? The wind that they create reaching for the butterfly often pushes the butterfly away.

The risks are the same when you are pushing the person you are having a conversation with too hard. Instead, you need to detach yourself from the outcome. Ensure that you keep a healthy amount of detachment from it. Your mental and emotional health should not be dependent on the other individual changing their mind about something.

Understand that this is the first attempt and not the last opportunity that you will have to talk to the person. You are learning, understanding, and collecting information that will be helpful to you in the next conversation, and the following conversations.

Issue a reminder if the boundaries you have set are crossed

Someone might forget to follow the rules of the conversation when they get so caught up in rapid-fire replies. When this happens, you can let them know about it and give them another chance.

If the individual's problematic behavior remains, mute or block them

If you have to cut anybody off if the conversation is getting abusive, do not feel bad about it. Tell them that you are cutting them off and let them know why you are doing it. Also, tell them that you are leaving the door open and they are welcome back if they become ready to converse in a productive way.

Recognizing Emotional Manipulation

Emotional manipulators use tactics such as twisting facts and bullying to exploit a relationship to their own benefit. Setting boundaries can help you in this situation. Emotional manipulators often seize power in a relationship through the use of mind games. Their goal is to control the other individual through the use of that power.

A relationship that is healthy is based on mutual respect, understanding, and trust. This is true of both professional and personal relationships. Sometimes, individuals exploit these elements of a relationship for their own benefit. It can be hard to identify the signs of emotional manipulation, as they can be subtle. They are usually difficult to identify, especially when you are the one experiencing the emotional manipulation. That does not make it your fault. No individual deserves to be emotionally manipulated. When you learn to recognize the emotional manipulation, you can put an end to it. Your sanity and self-esteem will also be protected.

Here are some common forms of emotional manipulation:

They use your weaknesses against you

They can use your weak spots against you when they know what they are. They may say and do things that are meant to upset you and leave you feeling vulnerable.

For instance, "You have always said that you would never want your children to grow up in a broken home. See what you are putting them through now." "This is a difficult audience. I would be scared if I was in your position."

They share too much too quickly to get close

Emotional manipulators may share their vulnerabilities and darkest secrets with someone too quickly to get close to them. This means that they skip a few steps in the early phase of a relationship. What they are doing with this tactic is to make you feel special to the point that you relax and divulge your secrets. These sensitivities can be used against you later.

For instance, "No one has ever shared their vision with me in the manner you have. I feel like we are meant to work on this together." I feel like we share a really deep connection. This has never happened to me before."

They make you feel guilty for your feelings

If you are sad, an individual who is manipulating you may try to accuse you of being unreasonable and make you feel guilty for feeling sad. The individual may accuse you of not being adequately invested.

For instance, "I couldn't accept that job. I would like to stay close to my children." "You would never question my decision if you really cared about me."

They may also talk about you to your colleagues behind your back.

For instance, "I would have loved to discuss this with you, but I am aware you are busy." "Since we are not very close, I thought it would be better if another individual said it to you."

They may communicate with you through people around you

They are passive-aggressive and may sidestep confrontation. Rather than communicating with you directly, they may communicate with you through the individuals around you, like your friends.

They always appear too calm, especially during periods of crisis

Manipulative people usually react in an opposite manner to the individual they are manipulating. This happens especially in situations that are emotionally charged so that they can use your reaction or response to make you feel sensitive. What happens is that you check your reaction and theirs and then come to the conclusion that you were the person out of line.

For instance, "I wanted to keep quiet about it, but you appeared to be a little out of control." You saw that every other person was quiet and calm. You were just too upset."

They use silent treatment to gain control over you

They do not respond to your direct messages, calls, or emails. They make you feel guilty for the wrong behavior they have displayed and use silence to gain control.

They use ultimatums or guilt trips

When a fight or disagreement is going on, a manipulative individual will try to put you in a difficult spot by making dramatic statements. They will aim to elicit an apology by using inflammatory statements to target emotional weaknesses.

For instance, "If you cannot be available next weekend, I think it represents your level of dedication to this project." "If you break up with me, I don't deserve to live."

They make you begin to question your sanity

Gaslighting is when someone tries to make you believe that your experience and instincts can no longer be trusted. It is a method of manipulation where you are made to believe that you are only imagining when those things actually happened. You are made to lose a sense of reality.

For instance, "I did not come late. You just did not remember what time I said I would come there." Everybody knows this doesn't work that way."

They do or say something and then completely deny it later

They use this technique to make you doubt yourself and question your memory of what happened. When you start having doubts about what actually happened, they can blame the issue on you, thereby making you feel that you are the cause of the problem.

For instance, "I never told you that. You are starting to imagine things" "I wouldn't commit to doing that. You know I have too many commitments."

You may not easily realize that you are being emotionally manipulated, and it may take a long time before you find out. The signs of emotional manipulation are subtle, and these signs usually evolve with time.

But you need to trust your instincts if you think that you are being emotionally manipulated. Apologize for what you have done to contribute to it and then move on. You may not even get an apology, but that should not bother you. Accept your part and then don't bring up the other accusations.

Ensure that you don't try to play this game and beat them at it. Instead, you must learn to recognize the strategies used for it as you will be able to properly get your responses ready.

Ensure that you set boundaries. When an individual who is manipulative discovers that they are starting to lose control, their desperation may increase. At this point, you need to make some difficult decisions. Consider cutting the person out of your life completely if you don't have to be close to them. If the individual is someone you work closely with or live with, it will be helpful to learn techniques that you will use for managing them.

Seeking guidance from a counselor or therapist will be helpful as they will guide you on how to manage the situation. They can help to open your eyes and you will be able to recognize dangerous patterns. They can then show you appropriate ways to confront the particular behavior and stop it. It is also helpful to get a trusted family member or friend to help you identify the particular behavior and then you can enforce boundaries.

Nobody deserves to be treated in this way by another individual. Emotional manipulation is capable of having a long-lasting effect on an individual even if it doesn't leave physical scars. Understand that anyone can heal from this and also learn and grow from it.

Importance of Emotional Intelligence

We all know that it is not individuals who are the smartest that are the most fulfilled or most successful in life. You may have seen individuals who are academically brilliant but are not successful in their personal relationships, are not successful at work, and are socially inept. Your intelligence quotient (IQ) or intellectual ability is not all that is needed to achieve success in life. Although a person's IQ can help them get into college, their EQ is what will make them successfully manage their emotions and stress during their final exams. EQ and IQ are both important.

The following areas of your life can be affected by emotional intelligence:

Your social intelligence and relationships
When you are in tune with your emotions, it connects you to other individuals and the world around you. You are able to reduce stress,

recognize friends from foes, use social communication to balance your nervous system, measure another individual's interest in you, and feel happy and loved with social intelligence. When you have a better understanding of your emotions and master how to control them, it will be easier for you to express your feelings and understand other people's feelings. This helps you to build stronger relationships both in your personal life and at work as it increases effective communication.

Your physical and mental health

If you find it hard to control your emotions, your stress is probably not being managed as well. This can cause serious health issues. When stress is not properly controlled, it can increase blood pressure, contribute to infertility, suppress the immune system, speed up the process of aging, and increase a person's risk of having a heart attack and stroke. An individual needs to first learn how to manage stress if they want to improve their emotional intelligence.

When emotions are uncontrolled and you are stressed, your mental health can be affected, making you vulnerable to depression and anxiety. If you find it difficult to understand, manage your emotions, or get comfortable with people, it will be hard for you to build strong relationships. This has the ability to leave you feeling isolated and further worsen any mental health issues.

Your work or school performance

High emotional intelligence has the ability to help you motivate and lead people, navigate the complexities of the workplace, and become successful in your career. Many companies employ EQ testing before hiring for jobs as they consider emotional intelligence as important as technical ability.

Increasing Emotional Intelligence

An individual's emotional intelligence, which is also referred to as their EQ or emotional quotient is the ability of the individual to understand their emotions and use the emotions in a variety of positive ways to empathize with others, communicate effectively, defuse conflict, relieve stress, and overcome challenges. It is helpful in building stronger relationships and helps people achieve their personal and career goals and achieve success at work and school. It has the ability to help individuals connect with their feelings, make informed decisions about what they are mainly concerned about, and take action.

EQ is as important as IQ when it comes to success and happiness in life. When you boost your emotional intelligence, you will easily form stronger relationships, and accomplish your goals.

You can learn the skills that make people have emotional intelligence at any time you want. However, you need to remember that learning about EQ and using that knowledge in your life are two different things. Although you are aware that you should do a particular thing, it doesn't always mean that you will do that thing, especially when stress overwhelms you, and this can override your good intentions. If you want to make permanent changes to your behavior such that it withstands pressure, you need to master how to overcome stress in your relationships and in the moment, in order to stay aware emotionally.

Emotional intelligence has four attributes. Self-awareness, social awareness, self-management, and relationship management are skills that will help you develop your EQ and help you manage your emotions and connect with other people.

Here are the key skills for building emotional intelligence:

The self-awareness attribute

The first step to developing emotional intelligence is managing stress. Your early life experience can influence your current emotional experience and attachment style. Your ability to handle core feelings such as fear, sadness, anger, and joy depends on the steadiness and quality of your early emotional experiences. If you had a primary caretaker when you were an infant who valued and understood your emotions, there is a high probability that your emotions will be valuable in your adulthood. But, if you had confusing, threatening, or painful emotional experiences as an infant, you most likely have tried to keep yourself away from your emotions.

Having the ability to connect to your emotions and having a close moment connection with your changing emotional experience is important for understanding how your actions and thoughts are influenced by emotions.

Do you often experience feelings that flow, moving from one emotion to another as there are changes in your experiences from moment to moment?

Do physical sensations that you have in places like your chest, throat, or stomach accompany your emotions?

Do you have individual emotions and feelings, such as fear, joy, anger, and sadness, each of which can be seen in facial expressions that are subtle?

Can you experience feelings that are intense and strong enough to capture your attention and other people's attention?

Do you focus on your emotions? Do they contribute to the decisions you make?

If you are not paying attention to your emotions, you may have even turned them down. If you want to become emotionally healthy and develop your EQ, you need to reconnect to your core emotions, embrace those emotions, and be comfortable with them. Practicing mindfulness can help you achieve this.

Mindfulness involves purposely staying focused on the present moment and paying attention to it without judgment. If you are preoccupied with a thought, mindfulness helps you shift from the state of preoccupation with that thought toward a state of showing appreciation for the moment and your emotional and physical sensations and gives you a larger perspective on life. Mindfulness focuses and calms you, thereby increasing your self-awareness.

You need to first learn how to manage stress if you want to develop your emotional awareness. This will make you more comfortable reconnecting to unpleasant or strong emotions and making changes to the way you respond to and experience your feelings.

You recognize your own emotions and how those emotions affect your behavior and thoughts. You are aware of your weaknesses and your strengths. You are also confident.

The social awareness attribute

Social awareness helps you recognize the mainly nonverbal cues other individuals are constantly using to communicate with you and interpret them. These cues help you know what is important to others, their changing emotional state, and how they are feeling.

You have empathy. You are able to understand other people's needs, emotions, and concerns, and you can recognize the power dynamics in an organization or group, you are able to feel comfortable socially, and you can pick up on emotional cues.

When similar nonverbal cues are sent out by groups of people, it makes you able to read the cues and understand the shared emotional experiences and power dynamics of the group. You are socially comfortable and empathetic. An ally of social and emotional awareness is mindfulness. The importance of mindfulness in the social process needs to be recognized to develop social awareness. After all, when you are zoning out on your phone, thinking about other things, or simply in your own head, it will be difficult for you to pick up on subtle nonverbal cues. You need to be present in the moment to be socially aware.

Although a lot of us are happy about the ability to multitask, what this means is that you won't notice the subtle emotional shifts going on in other individuals that make it easy for you to completely understand them. Your social goals will more likely progress further when you put your thoughts aside and stay focused on the interaction itself. When you are following the flow of another individual's emotional responses, it requires that you also focus on the changes taking place in your emotional experience as the process is a give-and-take process. Your self-awareness is not diminished when you pay attention to other people. When you put in effort and time to pay attention to other individuals, you will gain more understanding of your own beliefs, values, and emotional state. For instance, if hearing other people express certain views makes you uncomfortable then it has opened your eyes to something important about yourself.

The self-management attribute

You manage your emotions in healthy ways, control impulsive behaviors and feelings, adapt to changing circumstances, and follow through on commitments that you have started.

If you want to be able to engage your EQ, you must learn how to make constructive decisions about your behavior by using your emotions. Too much stress can make you unable to control your emotions and find it difficult to act appropriately and thoughtfully.

Has there been any time in your life when you have been overwhelmed with stress? Were you able to think clearly or stay away from making an irrational decision? It must have been difficult to do this. When stress overwhelms you, your ability to properly assess your emotions and other people's emotions and to think clearly becomes compromised.

Emotions are important when it comes to telling you about yourself and other individuals, but that leads us out of our comfort zone when we are stressed. Emotions can overwhelm us, making us unable to control ourselves. When you are able to manage your stress and remain present emotionally, you can master receiving information that is upsetting without allowing it to affect your self-control and thoughts. You will easily make choices that give you the opportunity to control impulsive behaviors and feelings, take initiative, manage your emotions in healthy ways, be able to adjust to different situations, and carry out promises.

The relationship management attribute

You know what to do to develop good relationships and maintain them. You also know how to manage conflict, work well in a team, communicate effectively, and influence and inspire others.

Your ability to recognize other people's feelings and understand their experiences helps you work well with people. Emotional awareness is important when working with people is concerned. You can successfully develop additional emotional and social skills that will help you form more fruitful, effective, and fulfilling relationships.

You need to become aware of your nonverbal communication and how effectively you use it. You may be sending nonverbal messages to people about your feelings and thoughts. The facial muscles, especially those around the forehead, nose, eyes, and mouth, help you to read other people's emotional intent and convey your own emotions without using words. The emotional area of the human brain is always on and other people won't ignore the messages it is sending even if you ignore the messages. Your relationships can be greatly improved when you start paying attention to and recognizing the nonverbal messages you are sending to other individuals.

Relieve stress with the use of play and humor. Play, laughter, and humor naturally ease stress. Your burdens are reduced and things are kept in perspective. Your nervous system is brought into balance, your stress is reduced, you calm down, your mind sharpens, and your empathy increases with laughter.

Ensure that you see conflict as an opportunity that can help you to grow closer to others. Disagreements and conflict are inevitable in relationships. Two individuals can't possibly have the same expectations, opinions, and needs every time. And having the same or different expectations, opinions, and needs, should not be a bad thing. Trust can be strengthened when conflict is resolved in constructive and healthy ways. Safety, creativity, and freedom in relationships are encouraged when conflict is not seen as punishing or threatening.

CHAPTER THREE:
Dark Psychology Techniques

Mind control, gaslighting, manipulation, and persuasion are some common dark psychology examples. Gaslighting involves distorting or denying reality and blaming an individual, making them doubt their own memories, perceptions, and sanity. Brainwashing, hypnosis, and cult indoctrination, which are used to change people's behaviors, values, and beliefs through intense cognitive and emotional manipulation, are all techniques of mind control.

Persuasion techniques involve convincing individuals to do something they don't intend to do by appealing to their needs, emotions, and desires. The individuals can be persuaded to join a group or buy a product even though they don't have the intention to do that.

Manipulation involves influencing the decisions and actions of individuals through the use of shame, fear, guilt, or some other negative emotions. Dark psychology works by exploiting people's biases, vulnerabilities, and cognitive limitations.

Here are some strategies and techniques used in dark psychology:

- Social influence involves persuading individuals to adopt certain behaviors or attitudes through the use of authority, peer pressure, or conformity.

- Emotional manipulation involves influencing people's behaviors through the use of emotions such as anger, sympathy, fear, or love.

- Power and control involve shaping people's behavior through the use of rewards, threats, or punishment to assert dominance over them.

- Cognitive distortions involve shaping the perceptions and beliefs of individuals through the use of misinformation, logical fallacies, or selective attention.

- Lies and deception involve confusing and misleading people through the use of omission, half-truths, or false information.

Persuasion Techniques

Persuasion is one technique that is often used in dark psychology to influence the decisions and behaviors of individuals. Persuasion techniques are used in interactions, personal relationships, marketing, and advertising. They are used to convince people to adopt a certain idea, belief, or behavior.

Let us take a look at some techniques of persuasion often used in dark psychology:

The brainwashing process.
Brainwashing involves various psychological techniques that are used to force a person to adopt a new set of values and beliefs. It is a process of indoctrination.

The scarcity technique.
This is a technique of persuasion where a person has a high likelihood of doing a certain thing if they believe it is limited or rare.

Influencing through subliminal messaging.
This technique is used to send hidden messages to people to influence their beliefs or behavior without their conscious awareness, and the messages are usually sent through sounds or images.

The social proof persuasion technique.

This is a persuasion technique where a person has a high likelihood of adopting a particular behavior or belief if they notice that other individuals are adopting it.

Influencing with hypnosis.

Hypnosis involves making people more susceptible to suggestion and influence by using a trance-like state.

The consistency technique.

This is a technique of persuasion where a person has a high likelihood of complying with a behavior or request if it matches with their previous beliefs or actions.

The authority technique.

Authority is a technique of persuasion where a person has a high likelihood of complying with a command or request if a perceived authority figure is issuing the command or request.

Manipulating with mind control.

Individuals or groups often use mind control techniques to manipulate and influence people by altering their thoughts, beliefs, and perceptions. They often use the techniques to exert power over others. Subliminal messaging, brainwashing, and hypnosis are some common techniques of mind control.

The reciprocity persuasion technique.

The reciprocity persuasion technique occurs when a person feels like they are obligated to reciprocate a gesture, so it makes them comply with a request. Reciprocity promotes relationships. And even though it exposes individuals to manipulation, it is a blessing and a curse. Sociopaths as well as other persuasive people use reciprocity. Hopefully, you will use the power of reciprocity for good. Understanding the power behind this principle is important.

Reciprocity is used by cult leaders, politicians, and many others to manipulate people and achieve their goals. These manipulators have commonalities that marketers and businesses should pay attention to. They include real or apparent conviction that they uphold the way and the truth. They include the determination to recruit other individuals by any means because they know the importance of having followers who are committed. They also include acknowledging that a little gift makes room for a large return favor because people are wired that way, and cultures also work that way.

There are people who might decide to hand out candies to people at a shopping mall during the Christmas season and then ask for donations in return. Our humanly biased response and the power of reciprocity make it possible for such people to receive donations far more than they would get if they didn't hand out any preceding gift.

Politicians use the power of reciprocity all the time. They use it with other techniques to manipulate people. They have the conviction and then they do everything possible within their power to mount an unassailable case for the way they have chosen so that their people would be logically and emotionally convinced of their action's necessity. They may acknowledge that their government has done something that was a mistake and they feel the need to atone for it with a gift. This makes the people accept the cost they are all paying for the things the government has failed to provide. The impact of the gift is powerful.

If used wisely, the principle of reciprocity can do wonders for you. It is formulated to make individuals feel a sense of obligation which makes them not follow their own decisions and then they do what favours you. This principle works whether you have good intentions or not.

Therefore, it is important that you ask yourself if you are manipulating people into making decisions that will harm them or if you are offering them something that will be valuable to them. As a person of integrity or a business owner with integrity, you have the responsibility to ensure you are not harming people in the process.

There are some products and services that are not ready to be sold at any price, and this is the truth. If that is the kind of product or service you are intending to offer, then you need to clean up your act. There are some products and services that the right customer will find useful.

As a person who sells, you should have a system for identifying buyers who are qualified because your reputation is involved. A business that is needy will take just any customer or client, and an ethical business will not just take any client. They will be ready to turn down any client that is not a good fit for them and stick to genuine standards that they have set for qualification.

When you understand that your gift will open the door, it makes you careful about the people you are targeting. You can use takeaway offers to disarm buyers. Although you may not be destructively manipulative in the marketing pitch you use, you may not be acknowledging that your offer is not meant for everybody and letting those who won't benefit know that. Qualified buyers are convinced that your offer is genuine. Another basic human instinct is also appealed to. This instinct is the desire of humans to have what they cannot get.

Sometimes, we are manipulated by the rule of reciprocity as people usually like to do favors for those they like. You may use the rules of psychology to your advantage and it may also work against you. Once you are aware of the rules, you will be able to tell when a person is trying to use the power of psychology against you. Anybody can use the rules of psychology against you if you don't know the rules. Once they see any opportunity, they will take advantage of you. Understanding the rules will help you know more about yourself, understand your way of thinking, and protect yourself from being manipulated.

One psychological rule that we have been victims of is the rule of reciprocity. People will usually feel indebted to repay the favor if you do something for them. This is how the reciprocity rule works. We have been told that it is our obligation to return the favor when somebody gives us something. You will be forever indebted to the person if you fail to return the favor. You don't want to be forever indebted to someone, do you? Besides, returning the favor is your obligation, right?

The manipulators are aware of this and usually take advantage of this tendency of humans to return the favor at every opportunity they get. These manipulators know that people will often fall for this and they are right about that. Even individuals who are very smart often fall for the reciprocity rule. They are aware of the rules, but they still fall for it.

Because humans are innately selfish, we instantly like someone who gives us a gift or does us a favor for nothing in return. There is a high likelihood of us doing a favor for someone we like. The reciprocity rule is more than just liking a person. It involves liking a person for a favor they have done for us and feeling indebted to the person for the favor. You feel obligated to repay the person's favor. Returning the favor is what society considers good behavior. Society thrives this way. When someone no longer uses the rule of reciprocity for the greater good but to manipulate or take advantage of someone, it can become an issue.

Tricks of Dark Psychology

The lying trick.
Lying may work and it may not work. It is a planned deception that works in the liar's favor. It can also involve exaggeration or partial truth. The communicator may recount a fictitious version of a situation.

The reverse psychology trick.
A person using reverse psychology advises someone to do a

particular thing one way, but they are aware the person will do that thing the other way. The manipulator intended for the person to do the opposite of what they have asked them to do.

The love flooding trick.

An example of love flooding is when you compliment or praise someone to encourage them to do something that you want them to do. When you apply love flooding to make someone feel wonderful, it will make them more likely to assist you with something you want them to do. If you want them to help you move some stuff around in your home, they will be more likely to help you do that.

A dark manipulator also has the ability to make a person feel attached to them, thereby making them do things that they wouldn't normally do.

The love denial trick.

Love denial includes withholding devotion and affection until you get what you want from the victim. The victim may find this very hard because they may feel that you have abandoned them and they may feel lost. When you ignore someone or give them the silent treatment until they give you what you desire, you are using this trick.

Understanding Body Language

Body language is used to give our message more impact and reveal our true feelings. It is the nonverbal part of communication. Communication is more than words. Nonverbal cues such as posture, gestures, and tone of voice all play their part.

An example of body language is a facial expression that is relaxed and becomes a genuine smile. Also, it can be a head tilt showing that you are thinking, arm and hand movements to demonstrate directions, or an upright stance to show interest. It can also be tapping your feet restlessly or taking care to avoid an arms-crossed posture that is defensive. When you are able to read these signs, you will be able to fully understand what a person is telling you. Your awareness of people's reactions to the things that you☐say and do will increase. And you will know how to adjust your body language so that you can appear more approachable, engaging, and positive.

Understanding how to interpret the body language of people to understand them and communicate with them more effectively will help you greatly in your personal and professional relationships.

An individual's body language is more important than their choice of words and tone of voice when communicating their true feelings. When you are aware of people's body language, it means that you are able to pick up on unspoken reactions and emotions. Reading people's body language is important, but you can miss it if you don't know what to look out for.

So, let us take a look at the most important nonverbal clues.

Examples of Negative Body Language

If an individual is exhibiting these negative behaviors, they will be unhappy, disinterested, and disengaged.

- If an individual has their eyes downcast or they are maintaining very little contact.
- If their arms are folded in front of their body.
- If their body is turned away from you.
- If they have tense or minimal facial expressions.
- Biting of nails, which suggests stress or insecurity.
- Fidgeting, which suggests that a person is distracted or disinterested.
- Blinking rapidly indicates concern or uncertainty.
- Locked ankles are also connected to anxious thoughts.

- Tapping/drumming fingers, which is often a sign of boredom or impatience.

When you are dealing with dissatisfied customers or people who are upset, you may encounter these negative behaviors.

When you are aware of the meaning of these signals, it can help you make adjustments to what you say as well as how you say it. When someone is not happy, you can show empathy for their unhappiness. For example, you can work to calm a situation that is heated or you can explain yourself more clearly.

If a person shows these signs during a negotiation, your focus should be on putting the person at ease and engaging their interest. Then, if the person stops displaying negative behavior, you will know that they are more open to persuasion and are ready to negotiate effectively with you.

Some types of body language show that a person is bored by what you are telling them. This might be in a one-on-one chat, a team meeting, or a presentation.

Some popular signs of boredom include:

- Doodling or writing.
- Picking at clothes, fidgeting, or fiddling with phones and pens.
- Gazing into space, or at something else.
- Sitting slumped, with head downcast.

You can fix this by inviting the person to contribute an idea or by asking them a direct question.

Examples of Positive Body Language

Individuals also convey positive feelings through their body language. The positive feelings can include happiness, interest, and trust. Seeing these signs lets you know that others are engaged with what you are telling them and they are at ease with the situation.

When you adopt these behaviors, you will be able to avoid sending mixed signals, convey your ideas more clearly, and support your points.

Here is how you can use positive body language effectively:

Making a good first impression.
Your body language plays a big role in the first impression people have of you. You can appear engaged trustworthy, calm, and confident, by doing the following:

Avoid fiddling with your hair, touching your face, or scratching your nose.
If you are answering questions and doing this, it might be taken as a sign of dishonesty. You need to convey trustworthiness, so avoid doing any of that. Sincere smiles are infectious, reassuring, and attractive.

Your posture should be open.
You should be relaxed and ensure that you don't slouch. Sit upright or stand upright and your hands should be placed by your sides. Ensure that you don't put your hands on your hips while standing, as this can communicate a desire to dominate and it can also communicate aggression.

Give a firm handshake, but ensure that you don't overdo it.
It should not become aggressive, awkward, or painful for the other individual.

Maintain eye contact for a few seconds.

When you maintain eye contact, it will help the other person know that you are engaged and sincere. Don't overdo it to avoid making it a staring contest. Hold their gaze for a few seconds at a time.

CHAPTER FOUR:
Dark Psychology and Hypnosis

So, you have the desire to hypnotize someone, but are not sure about how to do that? How can you successfully hypnotize someone? Well, hypnotizing someone isn't just about clicking your fingers and asking someone to sleep. There is a lot you need to understand about hypnosis.

How do you choose the person to hypnotize? You have a desire and you need someone to fulfil it. You can't hypnotize someone who doesn't want to be hypnotized. If an individual doesn't want to be hypnotized, they will most likely not go into hypnosis when you try to hypnotize them. So, you first need an individual who wants to be hypnotized. So, no matter how good you are with hypnosis, you don't have to hypnotize someone against their will.

After finding the person to hypnotize, you need to ensure that they are the right individual to hypnotize and you can safely hypnotize them. Some individuals are not as safe as others when hypnosis is involved and some others should not undergo hypnosis at all. Ensure that the individual you have chosen to hypnotize doesn't have personality disorders, dementia, psychosis, psychological disorders, brain trauma, uncontrolled epilepsy/seizures, severe clinical depression, and severe cognitive deficits/learning difficulties. Avoid hypnotizing anyone with any of the conditions we have mentioned, for their safety.

Once you have someone that you want to hypnotize, you need to find a location to use. You must have heard that a completely silent and comfortable environment is needed for hypnosis to be successful. You need to find a place where you will not have interruptions when you are starting out. You need to set up for success by ensuring comfort and fewer distractions during the process.

Once you are with the person you want to hypnotize, you can start by doing a pre-talk. This will help them relax and ensure they are comfortable before you start. An individual who is not relaxed or who has other things on their mind will probably not go into hypnosis. You can start the pre-talk by asking them what are their thoughts. You can also find out if the individual has any concerns before you start the process. It will also be helpful to ask about their previous experience as it can positively or negatively affect the hypnosis.

The Process of Hypnosis

Progressive relaxation induction is a common method of inducing a state of hypnosis. However, there are a variety of other kinds of hypnotic induction. For progressive relaxation induction, you give the individual "suggestions" to help them relax their mind and body progressively. This can take only a few minutes and not hours. Before the hypnosis begins, you need to first consider how you will deliver the relaxing suggestions. Your voice should portray relaxation and convey confidence. So, ensure that your voice sounds relaxing and confident when you are ready to start with your hypnotic suggestions.

You can begin by asking the individual to take three deep breaths and then proceeding to ask them to close their eyes. Once the person has closed their eyes, direct suggestions can continue, which can include feeling calm, breathing slowly, and relaxing as your voice makes them feel comfortable. Repetition is important. You can use similar suggestions repeatedly and use them slightly differently sometimes. You can make suggestions that the individual starts to relax their muscles, beginning at their feet and moving up through the whole of their body. The next thing is to make suggestions that they imagine themselves going down a staircase of 15 steps, and that each step taken is making them feel more relaxed.

You need to give the individual enough time to listen to your suggestions and comply with them, so even though you may feel like rushing through the suggestions, take it slowly and give them enough time to respond. You are trying to make them feel relaxed, so you need to feel relaxed as well.

After getting the person to a relaxed state, the individual should be in a state of hypnosis. Some individuals remain light throughout the process, while others go deep into hypnosis. Once the person is hypnotized, you can then do what you want. They will respond to the suggestions you give, whether they are for entertainment or therapy. Individuals who are deeply hypnotized and responsive may be able to easily respond to hypnotic suggestions and engage in more complex therapy techniques under your direction.

It is easy to wake the individual from hypnosis. You only need to inform them that you will count from 1 to 5, and then they will wake up. You can give them suggestions to get more alert, awake, and energized. Ensure that you give the individual suggestions that will make them feel really good when they wake up.

Controlling the Mind with Hypnosis

You can control someone's mind using mind control techniques and get them to follow your orders. Hypnosis techniques can make an individual do what you want them to do as the techniques help you hijack the conscious mind of the individual. When hypnotized, many individuals do things they have no memory of and things they wouldn't have done. Putting a person in a trance and making suggestions to them to get them to do what you want them to do is mind control. Many individuals have been victims of mind control techniques.

Hypnosis is not just a trick of showmen and magicians. It is used in the treatment of addictions. People also use it to forget about their psychological fears and overcome their bad habits. Burn victims and patients experiencing immense pain caused by grievous accidents

47

and cancer have been treated with this technique and it has been known to reduce the intensity of their discomfort and control their pain. Studies show that it greatly reduces the feeling of pain.

People use this technique to help them easily lose weight and overcome their food cravings. Hypnosis also helps pregnant women overcome their labor pain and give birth to the baby easily. In addition to the medical uses of hypnosis, a few speculative uses also exist. Many skilled hypnotics use the techniques to persuade individuals to do what they are not even aware that they are doing. The person completely follows only the voice of the person. Many people have used hypnosis to make individuals hand over money without resistance or to sign the papers to a property. Kidnappers have even used hypnosis to hypnotize kids and take them away. Some individuals have been hypnotized into murdering someone and some have been hypnotized and sexually abused.

This means that hypnosis can be dangerous and useful at the same time. But, is it possible to use the techniques of hypnosis in your daily life to achieve your desires? Can you convince your child to stay focused on their studies, make someone fall in love with you, or make your boss at work to allow you close from work early every day? Well, it is possible to achieve things in life through the use of mind control.

You use hypnosis every day without being aware that you are even using it. This may even be happening to you when you like someone and find yourself often following them. So, if you notice that you follow your friend to go out for dinner or a movie without thinking about it when you are meant to stay at home and study for an exam you have the next day, hypnosis could be involved. If a person likes you, they may do whatever you want just to make you happy. Thus, you may have said yes to doing something you don't want to do simply because you are attracted to the person asking you to do them that favor or you like the person. This may have happened to you many times.

But what if the person is a complete stranger, like a prospective client or a salesperson? If this is the case, you need to use mind control techniques that involve mirroring the behavior of people. The answer can be found in watching the individual carefully and picking up some repetitive words or actions that they use. Ensure that you use the same actions or words during your interactions with that individual, and they will get to see the similarities you have with them, and this will make them develop a rapport with you.

Controlling Minds through Stories

Have you noticed that individuals get engrossed when watching movies or reading a story that is interesting and try to copy the character that made the most impact in their minds? So, while having conversations with people every day, include some short anecdotes in those conversations that will make it possible to control the other person's mind. Negative sentences can even help you make someone do what you want them to do. Reverse psychology is like this. You tell the individual that they don't need to do a particular thing right now and then they go ahead and do that thing immediately. And this is actually what you want them to do.

When asking people to do something, ensure that you choose your words carefully, as individuals often imagine an image of what you said they should do. When you tell someone that they should not allow the glass case to drop, the person imagines it falling and may even imagine themselves making it fall. But if you ask them to transport it safely, chances are that they will do their best to transport it carefully.

You can try these techniques. You can learn hypnotism and get better at it over the years with practice. It is important that you know how to make an individual come out of a trance when you make them go under a trance. They should come out of trance without any negative consequences. Some hypnotics use a word, click, or clap to make an individual come out of a deep sleep or undergo a trance.

You are using hypnosis to make the subconscious mind more alert than the conscious mind.

You have no idea of what the individual has stored in their subconscious mind that may be harmful to them and you as well. So, ensure that you are careful when you are trying the techniques. You can try mind control techniques that are easier in your everyday life and make your partner return home early or get a good bargain for a product from a salesperson. Just make sure that the attractive man or woman sitting opposite you in the bar doesn't hypnotize you.

Achieving Your Goals with Self-Hypnosis

Have you watched television programs and horror films that portray hypnosis as something frightening that villains use to control the minds of helpless individuals and enslave them? You may have watched stage shows where it appears that a hypnotist used their "hypnotic powers" to make individuals say and do things these individuals would never say and do normally. So, hypnosis may appear wacky, like other mystical phenomena. Hypnosis is therapeutic and has the ability to help individuals overcome many physical, emotional, and psychological issues. When an individual is in a state of hypnosis, they are aware, in a natural state, and can come out of hypnosis when they wish to come out of it.

The hypnosis state is a state of highly focused attention with increased suggestibility. Relaxation does not always accompany hypnosis. When someone like a therapist, hypnotizes another individual, it is referred to as hetero hypnosis. This is often called hypnotherapy. Autohypnosis is when hypnosis is self-induced. This is often known as self-hypnosis.

The word hypnosis originates from "hypos," which is a Greek word, meaning sleep. Neuro-hypnotism is abbreviated. Neuro-hypnotism means the sleep of the nervous system.

However, an individual is awake when in hypnosis. They are not in a sleep state and are aware of all that is being done and said. People often use self-hypnosis to modify emotions, behavior, and attitudes. For example, many individuals deal with the daily problems of life with self-hypnosis. Self-hypnosis has the ability to help individuals develop new skills and boost their confidence. It proves beneficial for reducing anxiety and stress and can aid in overcoming habits like overeating and smoking. Sportsmen and women can use self-hypnosis to enhance their athletic performance, and hypnosis is also useful for individuals suffering from stress-related illnesses or physical pain. Before hypnosis can be used for stress-related illnesses or physical pain, a medical diagnosis has to be made and it has to be under a qualified therapist or doctor's guidance.

Technique for Self-hypnosis

Let us take a look at an effective self-hypnosis technique. This simple technique is effective and popular and is known as eye fixation self-hypnosis. It can help you relax. We will first use it for relaxation and then add hypnotic suggestions as well as imagery. Start by going into a room where you will not be distracted and then turn off your computer, television, or phone. This will help you reduce distractions. This time is yours and you will be focusing on nothing else but your goal of self-hypnosis.

Do the following:

1. Sit in a chair you are comfortable in and don't cross your legs and feet.

Ensure that you don't eat a large meal just before you start hypnosis to avoid feeling uncomfortable or bloated. Avoid lying on a bed as it will likely make you fall asleep. Sit in a comfortable chair so that you don't nod off. It is best to take off your shoes and wear clothing that is not too tight. It is also advisable to remove any contact lenses if you wear them. Avoid crossing your legs and feet.

51

2. Fix your gaze on the ceiling and breathe deeply.

Without tilting your neck to the back or straining your neck, look for a spot on the ceiling and keep your eyes on that spot. While you fix your gaze on that spot take in a deep breath and then breathe out. Ensure that you hold it for a moment before breathing out. Silently say the suggestion "I want to sleep now, my eyes are heavy." Continue repeating this process, and allow your eyes to close and then relax. When you are saying the suggestion, say it as if you mean it. You can say it in a convincing and soothing manner.

3. Allow your body to relax.

Free yourself and allow your body to become loose. The next thing to do is to slowly count down from ten to zero. Tell yourself that you are getting more relaxed with each and every count. Focus on your breathing while you remain in this relaxed state for some minutes. Be aware of how your diaphragm and chest are rising and falling. Pay attention to how your body is becoming relaxed without you even doing too much to relax it. In fact, your body becomes more relaxed the less you try to relax it.

4. Use visualization.

Visualize an image that stands for something you desire mastery of and see yourself accomplishing your goal.

5. Use positive suggestions.

Say a positive suggestion like "I am calm, confident, and relaxed" three times.

Say it to yourself with conviction while visualizing for about one minute the image of what you desire. Repeat this suggestion three times and ensure that you stay in hypnosis between times and also be focused on the relaxation of your body.

6. Come back to the room when you are ready by counting from one to ten.

Let yourself know that you are becoming aware of your

surroundings and you will open your eyes at the count of ten. Start counting up from one to ten in an energetic way. When you get to ten, you can then open your eyes and stretch your legs and arms. Practice the technique repeatedly up to four or five times and pay attention to how you become deeply relaxed each time.

If you try this technique and discover that it doesn't make you feel as relaxed as you would like, don't give up, and don't force it. You only need to continue practicing regularly to become better at it. Sometimes, individuals will feel drowsy after hypnosis. This is harmless and only takes a few seconds. It is just similar to how you feel when you wake up from an afternoon nap. Although this is harmless, ensure that you do not operate any machinery or drive until you are fully awake.

Post-Hypnotic Suggestions

Have you ever tried to remember a name and found yourself frustrated because you couldn't remember the name? The more you try to remember it, the harder it becomes. Then the name comes back to you later when you are relaxed. Sometimes, we block ourselves from accomplishing our goals when we try too hard. Your attitude towards self-hypnosis is what will determine if you will get better at it or not. Relax and don't set unrealistic goals. Set realistic goals and take your time. You may not be achieving results as fast as you want, but you should accept the pace at which things are going even though the results may seem small at first. Stop doubting yourself and believe you can do it. With time, you will accomplish your goal.

Hypnosis involves heightened suggestibility. When you give yourself suggestions during hypnosis, it will make a response or action take place after the hypnosis. The suggestions are known as post-hypnotic suggestions and they can make it possible for you to achieve your goals. As the years pass by, hypnotherapists have created suggestion rules.

The rules have been summarized below. They will help you achieve success with these suggestions:

1. Suggestions should be in the present tense and should be phrased positively.

Many people will not react more favorably to a negatively worded suggestion as much as they would react to a positively worded one. You will have more effective suggestions when you talk about what you want to move toward and not what you want to get away from. For instance, instead of saying, "I am not scared," you can say "I am calm."

Would you rather hear something like, "Would you mind doing this?" or "Do not say you won't do this."

It is better to say "I stop drinking alcohol with ease" instead of "I will try to stop drinking alcohol" because using the word try means that you are struggling to stop drinking alcohol and finding it hard to stop. It is better for your suggestions to be phrased as though they were taking place presently. They should be in the present tense.

So, it is better to say "I am relaxed in the car" instead of "I will be relaxed when I am in the car". Or you can say, "My confidence is increasing" instead of "I will try my best to be confident".

2. Say the suggestions as if you mean what you are saying.

How do actors perform? Have you ever seen any of them speaking in a quiet voice and mumbling their lines on stage? The performance will not be convincing. People often repeat hypnotic suggestions silently. It is not like acting. However, when repeating the suggestions, you need to say the suggestions as if you mean what you are saying. Be confident, positive, and reassuring.

3. Repetition is important.

Suggestions are valuable to advertisers, which is what makes them repeat radio and television commercials regularly. Repetition is an important rule when an individual is practicing self-hypnosis. This helps to drive the point home and make positive change.

4. Your suggestions should be realistic and specific.

You will have more effective suggestions if they are realistic and specific. If you have the desire to improve your basketball performance, you cannot unrealistically give the suggestion "I am a world-class basketball player," unless you are truly a world champion or are about to become one. Instead, find out what specific thing you wish to improve upon when it comes to the way you play basketball. So, if your desire is to improve a specific area of your basketball playing, you would give realistic suggestions that are specific to that part. Your suggestions should be structured based on the changes you can make in yourself that are within your control and not unrealistic things, such as external events, that are not within your control. Do not give suggestions for more than one issue at once. For example, when you use the suggestion "I am confident that I can stop smoking and lose weight," you will notice that it is not really effective. Instead, pick one goal at a time and work on it, repeating suggestions that are connected to that goal. Move ahead to the next goal you have after you see results.

Hypnosis and Imagery

Visualize the situation when you are giving yourself suggestions. Also, visualize your desired feeling and action. You can make use of your sense of hearing, touch, and smell, in addition to picturing an outcome that you desire. You can use images from your experiences and memories and also create new images. Individuals sometimes believe it is crucial to see a clear image of their goal. However, a belief that you are in line with your goal as well as a positive attitude is more important than having a clear image of your goal.

This exercise shows how effective imagery and suggestion can be.

Ensure that you avoid using it if you don't like lemons.

- Make yourself comfortable while sitting in a chair and close your eyes.
- Picture a lemon and imagine yourself cutting it into 2.
- Be aware of the lemon juice running down each lemon piece.
- Take a piece of the lemon and bite into it.

Even if you don't have a clear image of the lemon, you might still find your mouth watering and you might grimace.

Adding Visualization and Hypnotic Suggestion To Self-Hypnosis

Jenny is due to participate in a play, but she often experiences stage fright and is worried that her performance will be less than the standard of performance that she is capable of. Jenny wants to practice self-hypnosis to increase her confidence. In self-hypnosis and results imagery, the individual visualizes him or herself performing in the way he or she desires while at the same time repeating some post-hypnotic suggestions to accomplish a goal. After Jenny puts herself into hypnosis, she visualizes herself performing on stage with ease and confidence. She repeats the post-hypnotic suggestion "I am performing with confidence and ease" three times while visualizing herself for one minute. She does the visualization two more times while she is still in hypnosis.

Setting Your Goals for Self-Hypnosis

1. Get a book or paper and write your goals. Be specific and clear about what you want to do. Ensure that the goals you set are achievable. If the goals you have are long-term goals, you can break them down into manageable steps.

2. Prioritize achieving your goals. Decide to practice self-hypnosis every day and you will begin to see results.

3. Make a decision about the imagery you want to use. If your goal is to relax your body, visualize a beautiful scene like a park or a beach on a warm day. You can also use results imagery.

4. Write down the hypnotic suggestions you have formulated. Write out some suggestions to use for the goal that you want to accomplish. Abide by the post-hypnotic suggestions' rules. You can even create your own script that you will use.

5. Do not be too hard on yourself if you fail to accomplish a goal. Understand that failing to accomplish a goal does not make you a failure. You may need to stay persistent or even try a different approach towards the goal.

Reducing Anxiety and Relaxing Yourself with Self-Hypnosis

The script below will help you cope with anxiety and relax. You can alter the imagery to make it align with your needs. For example, you may choose to imagine yourself in a park on a warm day instead of visualizing yourself on a beach. You can also choose to change the symbolism used to address a situation that you desire to work on. You can record the text and replay it, or get an individual to read it to you.

You first need to become hypnotized as before by doing the following:

1. Sit in a place that is comfortable for you and then ensure that your legs and feet are uncrossed.

2. Without straining your neck or tilting your head, choose a point on the ceiling and keep your eyes on that spot. While your eyes are focused on that spot, breathe in deeply and hold it for some time as

long as you feel comfortable. Then while you are breathing out, you can say the suggestion "My eyes are heavy and tired and I want to sleep. Continue repeating the process a number of times and, if your eyes are yet to close, allow them to close and relax your eyes in a closed position.

3. Repeat this script with conviction and say it silently and with conviction:

"I am giving my body the opportunity to become loose and get comfortable in the chair. I am starting to notice the place in my body where the comfort is as I continue to relax. Perhaps I experience a comfortable feeling of warmth in my fingers and hands or maybe I notice the comfort in some other part of my body. The comfort deepens with every sound I hear and every breath I take. I now start counting down from ten to zero. I become more relaxed with each count."

"I now visualize myself on a beautiful beach and feel the sun's warmth on my body and the sand's warmth under my feet. I imagine myself alone by the beachside or that other individuals are also there as I continue to relax. I listen to the waves lapping against the seashore and the sound of the sea. I feel so relaxed, secure, and calm, and I feel that I can remain by the beachside for as long as I want to. After a few minutes, I visualize myself in a field on a warm summer's day. There is a hot air balloon in the middle of the field and a basket is attached to the balloon. The basket attached to the balloon is weighed down on the ground with the use of sandbags. The hot air balloon hangs in the sky effortlessly. I imagine myself placing my fears, worries, or anxieties into the basket. I feel more relief the more I offload my fears and anxieties into the basket. It feels as if I had been carrying a great weight which has now been lifted."

"I let the sandbags go and watch as the balloon and the basket move up into the air. I experience relief as I watch the balloon going up into the air. I feel more relief as the balloon rises higher. My worries and fears appear to be more insignificant as the balloon becomes more distant. As I continue to watch the balloon becoming smaller in the distance, I say the following to myself five times:

"I am releasing my fear, worries, and anxiety."

When ready to come out of hypnosis, I count up starting from one to ten, and then open my eyes. When you engage in self-hypnosis, the suggestions you give yourself and the imagery you use are only exposed to limits from your imagination.

You need to know the following:

- Hypnosis is used to overcome many emotional, psychological, and physical issues. It is therapeutic. It is not an unconscious state, a mystical state, or a state of sleep. When an individual is in hypnosis, they are aware and are able to come out of it when they want to. It is a harmless and natural state.

- When you want to practice self-hypnosis, ensure that you do not eat a large meal before starting the process as it can make you feel uncomfortable or bloated. Unless you want to doze, ensure that you sit in a comfortable chair and avoid lying down, as you might start feeling sleepy if you lie down. It is best to take off your shoes and loosen tight clothing. It is best to remove contact lenses if you wear them. Your legs and feet should not be crossed.

- Self-hypnosis is capable of modifying emotions, behavior, and attitudes. It can be beneficial for individuals to engage in activities that help them acquire new skills and enhance their self-assurance. It can also decrease anxiety and stress, and help individuals overcome habits such as overeating and smoking. Sportspeople also use self-hypnosis to enhance their athletic performance. It is essential to get advice from a competent therapist or a doctor before practicing self-hypnosis if you are facing any psychological or medical issues.

- Engage in self-hypnosis regularly. Take your time and relax. Even though you may seem to be achieving results slowly, you need to accept the pace. Your results may appear small initially, but you must believe in yourself and you will accomplish your goals and become successful in no time.

- Remember that failing to succeed in accomplishing a goal does not make you a failure. You may just need to stay persistent or approach the goal differently.

You can use the following post-hypnotic suggestions in your self-hypnosis and you can make them fit your needs:

My relaxation gets deeper every time I enter into hypnosis.

I am getting more confident and assertive when I have conversations with my colleagues.

It is easy for me to stop smoking.

I am secure, calm, and relaxed every day.

I eat healthy meals three times a day.

Every single day I embrace and accept myself just the way I am.

Hypnosis and Its Dark Side

People intentionally and unintentionally use hypnosis to do good and evil things. Ethically minded hypnosis practitioners need to acknowledge the following risks and protect themselves against them.

The intention.

The therapist's intention is important in terms of outcomes. Indeed, if a therapist sincerely wants to help someone, they can get a good result even if they are not technically hugely proficient. However, individuals who can put their egos completely aside are rare and therapists have egos too. Ego can cause a specific pitfall for some individuals who use hypnotherapy, as these individuals have discovered that they can easily put people into a trance, whereas, it appears to be a mysterious process for most people. These individuals might even have made themselves believe that immense skill is required, so it makes their egos puff up and this can negatively affect patients. Practitioners are often encouraged to use the term guided imagery instead of hypnosis for the sake of preventing misconceptions on the part of the client and the therapist.

Taking away an individual's sense of control.

Humans have the innate need to have a sense of control over their own lives. Therapists are not the ones to make assumptions about their client's needs. It is important that the changes the therapist is guiding the client to make are in accordance with the client's goals that they have clearly established beforehand. So, even when the client is in a state of trance, the goals are clearly understood by both the therapist and the client. Therapists should also give their clients the tools to cope without them, as fast as possible. Therefore, mastering effective brief techniques is important for therapists. Therapists can also teach their clients to relax and avoid becoming reliant on recordings that the therapists provide for them or on recordings that they might provide for them. Clients can use these until therapy is no longer needed.

Hallucinations.

When hallucination is induced, it can cause vulnerable people to have psychotic breakdowns. This is dangerous because an individual who is in a psychotic state cannot distinguish between the waking reality and the dream state as we usually do.

False memory syndrome.

There are families who have been pulled apart as a result of false memories of parental sexual abuse "uncovered" during therapy. Clinicians are being alerted to false memory syndrome. There are cases of people who have recalled some things in therapy that later emerged that they had been confabulating along with their therapists. So, it is important for therapists to be careful not to make suggestions that are emotionally arousing, even by asking questions, such as the possibility of abuse, childhood neglect, or that a spouse may be engaged in an affair, which their clients may dwell on and then dream about. The clients may then later recall the dream and without due evidence, give credence to it.

Telepathy.

When therapists are seriously trying to help an individual, they often go into a deeply focused state and, at such times, there can be a confusion of ego boundaries, thereby causing harm to both client and therapist. A field of relationship is involved every time we make a connection with another individual. A lot of therapists experience telepathy when it comes to their clients. For example, if a therapist wishes to have fewer clients on a particular day or if they feel that they have low energy, their clients will usually start to call them up to postpone appointments. This often happens and is quite too astonishing to be down to chance. One experience that is common is suddenly knowing that a person who is close has died, even if the person was in good health and miles away.

Using hypnotic words.

Political parties and cults practice hypnosis. For instance, when politicians use abstract hypnotic words like principles, values, or positive change, it forces individuals into an internal trance to attempt to search and understand what the words mean, even though no concrete examples are given by the politicians. Everybody has something that they want to change in their life. And nobody wants a change that is negative. So, using words like "progressive" or "change" by politicians is a con trick.

If you think hypnosis is harmless, you need to know that Hitler studied it after a hypnotist healed him of the hysterical blindness that he had at the end of World War 1. A strong suggestion that a psychologist gave him in a trance changed his personality. He was told that he had great personal powers and he was special. He was also told that he could use his great powers to cure himself of the blindness. This represented a post-hypnotic suggestion and vast crowds at rallies had receptive trance states induced in them by Hitler, thereby bombarding them with nominalizations that were emotionally arousing. A stylized form of arm levitation was even adopted as the Nazi salute by him.

In therapy, clients are sent on their own internal search to find meanings for strengths, creativity, inner resources, etc. through the use of abstract language with benign intentions, but remaining mindful of how unintended consequences can happen when language is used loosely as well as how power can easily be abused is important. If certain abstractions are not made concrete, overusing positive abstractions that induce trance can hinder a client from going forward. When therapists have clients that talk in abstract terms, the therapists may sometimes get entranced by the abstractions, do their own internal searches, and don't succeed when it comes to seeing past them. Getting seduced into a trance can be surprisingly easy, even when you believe that you know better.

Destroying an individual's very essence.
When hypnotic techniques are used to help an individual access the REM state, the individual's unique essence is being tapped into. A hypnotic induction involves trespassing upon the private mental territory of some other person's essence. We should only enter this territory respectfully if we are invited, and the gate must be carefully closed when we leave the territory. Continuous use of hypnosis on a person will weaken them, as it is capable of putting out the spark of volition by increasing their openness to suggestion, and also to the suggestions of others. For this reason, it is important for therapy to

be brief.

Therapy helps individuals detach and cope on their own, not depending on others. Severe cases of repeated hypnosis are capable of deranging the brain, as when ordinary people think of others as things and not as humans, and when they start acting in grotesque ways. When some people think it is acceptable to torture, kill, and rape people, it means that emotional arousal through chanting, repetition, fear, or other means has been used to hypnotize these people to make them become more suggestible. Hypnosis as well as the programming of people are used in all dangerous mass movements, once the people are emotionally aroused.

When an individual is bombarded with continuous regular hypnosis sessions, their mind can become powerless, thereby leading to mental asylum instead of gaining better control and power. A therapist cannot continue trying to bolster an individual who is psychologically damaged by telling them that they have a bright future and that they are desirable or they are talented, without any evidence at all, and doing nothing to make this actually a reality. People's spiritual and psychological development can be affected if hypnosis is used carelessly, and this can be called psychic murder.

CHAPTER FIVE:
Dark Psychology and Brainwashing

Brainwashing is the process whereby an individual's core values, beliefs, affiliations, and ideas are replaced, to the extent that the individual can't think critically or independently and has no control over themselves. Anyone can be brainwashed. This includes people who have been sacked from their workplace and have nothing to do, people who are suffering from an illness that needs to be cured by all means, people who have lost their loved ones through divorce or death, and people who have lost their homes and forced to start living on the streets. Even the most powerful and intelligent person can be brainwashed. You encounter brainwashing techniques every day and you can learn how to use them or avoid them. While it is unlikely that you may be deliberately targeted for brainwashing, you could be subject to some techniques related to the practice. You encounter these methods regularly and you can avoid them.

Mind control, which is also referred to as coercive persuasion, thought reform, brainwashing, thought control, or mind abuse, is a process in which a person or a group persuades other people to conform to their wishes through the use of manipulative methods, and this is often done to the detriment of the people being manipulated.

Brainwashing is a form of manipulation. It is usually associated with cults and people use it in everyday life. Brainwashing techniques are often leveraged by politicians, news networks, advertisers, and so on.

Here are some of the most notable brainwashing techniques:

- The individual is offered a number of choices by the

manipulator, but all the choices they have offered the individual leads to the same conclusion.

- The manipulator provides the victim with information on various subjects and they provide it in constant short snippets. This makes the information overwhelming for the victim and trains them to have a short-term memory. The victim highly desires the information that the manipulator is providing due to how highly overwhelmed the victim feels.

- There is repetition of the same phrase or idea to make sure that it sticks in the individual being manipulated's brain.

- The individual is put in a heightened state through emotional manipulation, making it more difficult for them to use logic. Inducing anger and fear are among the manipulated emotions that are the most common.

The Brainwashing Process

Someone who is trying to brainwash you will be intentional about knowing the details about your life so that they can use the information to manipulate your beliefs. They will want to know what your strengths are, who you confide in, what your weaknesses are, and who you consider important in your life and take advice from.

Here is the process of brainwashing:

The isolation tactic.
Isolation is the first tactic used in brainwashing someone because when your friends and family members are around you, your manipulators will not find it easy to manipulate you. The manipulator doesn't want someone with an idea that is different from theirs or a person who asks questions to first understand what the manipulator is trying to get them to do. This technique starts in the form of constantly checking where you are and who you are

spending time with, or preventing you from accessing your family or friends.

Introducing an alternative way of livelihood.
If you want to break down an individual and reshape the person in a different image, you must introduce an alternative way of their livelihood which is more attractive than the present one.

Breaking down self-esteem.
A person is easily brainwashed when they have low self-confidence and they are in a vulnerable condition. So, when the manipulator wants to brainwash an individual, they ensure that the person is in a vulnerable condition to enable them to carry out their plans. The manipulator can easily rebuild a broken person with their own beliefs. The manipulator breaks down the person's self-esteem by employing strategies like verbal abuse, physical abuse, sleep deprivation, embarrassment, or intimidation. A manipulator will start to control everything about the person's life, starting from the time they wake up in the morning to the time they sleep.

Blindly follow orders.
A manipulator's ultimate goal is to make the target follow their orders without asking any questions. Repeating a similar statement continuously is an effective way of controlling a person. When the same statement is repeated, it is perfect for halting the doubting thoughts. Research has shown that the repetitive and analytical parts of the mind are not interchangeable.

Humiliation and degradation.
You get more harmed by the brainwasher when you stand up for yourself, question their ideas, or resist their demands. When you get angry, the punishment you go through is more severe than just doing what they wanted you to do in the first place. The brainwasher will often use mere words to degrade you through abuse, and they will

humiliate you before friends or co-workers whenever they like. The humiliation degrades you and reduces your sense of self-worth.

Issuing threats.
The brainwasher threatens the victim that they will leave the relationship. The abuser also uses body language to deliver the threats.

Testing their target.
Brainwashers don't often think that they have completed their work, as there are times when their victim could start thinking for themselves again and then take back control of their life. When a brainwasher tests their target, it makes them see that they are still brainwashed and the brainwasher gets to understand how much control they have over the individual. They might ask their target to do something like a criminal act, for instance, robbing someone's store or burglarizing a home.

Prove that they know everything.
Most Brainwashers will use their friends, stalk you during relationships, or exploit coincidence to show that they are aware of everything you do even in their absence.

Perception Monopolization.
- The manipulator utters words that make you look deeper at yourself and start feeling vulnerable.

- The manipulator makes you unable to do things that are off-limits.

- The manipulator keeps you focused on them.

- The manipulator attempts to remove anything that they can't control from your life.

Brainwashers attempt to weaken your ability to resist their control by doing the following:

- They keep you always busy meeting the very high standards they have set for cleanliness, parenting, and holiness.

- They look for tactics to make you feel guilty for refusing to accept their demands.

- They may claim that you have a sub-par character and insist that you change it.

- They may add other tasks to your life that are a lot more than the tasks expected in a normal relationship.

- They may demand that you attend social events that will help with improvement in their professional career and they may demand that you become friends with their boss's partner.

Can a person overcome brainwashing and heal from it? Yes, it is possible. If you are aware that you have been brainwashed, you can still heal from the effects and improve from what domestic violence has caused you and take back control of your mind. First, you need to learn how the manipulator put you under their control through the use of brainwashing techniques.

Manipulating People

You will have times in your life when you don't get what you desire from people, but it doesn't mean you should be disappointed. Learn to manipulate the lemon salesperson when life gives you lemons. This is how to do it.

You need to understand that manipulating people can be generally a bad thing. You can learn how to do it and use it positively or use it to know when you are being manipulated in your daily interactions with people and protect yourself against the harm that manipulative people can cause.

Become a master of your emotions.

Ideally, the person you are targeting won't have so much control over their emotions, but that shouldn't make you lazy. You need to be able to act since you are a master manipulator. You will need to master important skills that may include getting angry when it suits your needs or shedding a tear. Whether you are looking for sympathy, you want to incite fear, or anything else you want to do, it will depend on the particular situation you want to handle. So, mastering your own emotions is important to enable you to have the right tools for the task at hand.

Logic and emotion.

Playing on people's emotions is the easiest way to manipulate them. If you give people enough time to think about something, they will likely make a logical decision. However, if you manipulate them into feeling a certain way that is of benefit to you, it will be easy for you to get what you want from them. This is known as emotional manipulation.

Learn to flirt often and be charming.

You can't just throw tantrums or cry like children do whenever you need something. You have to be likable. Charm is needed when it comes to manipulating individuals. If you are an individual who is ridiculously likable a lot of the time, reacting with extreme emotion will greatly impact the situation. When you are able to control your emotions, it means you don't just have the ability to act, but you can keep your emotions in check most of the time. Although a charming personality is great, having the ability to flirt can also be helpful. The target generally feels poorly when manipulated, whether they are aware that they are being manipulated or not. The more the target likes you, the better things will flow. Disregard your own sexuality's boundaries and some suggestive touches can be thrown in when you believe that they will be effective. Lonely individuals and those with low self-esteem often find this tactic effective.

Hide negative action in altruism.

Even if you are not a good person, you have to seem like you are. If there is ever a need to take a negative action like blaming someone else, whether it's the person's fault or yours, yelling at the target, or even criticizing behavior, you should do your best to wrap it in altruism. An altruist is not easily hated, so painting yourself as one is very effective. For instance, if your target didn't do what you wanted them to do and you yelled at them, you can frame the outburst as a way of helping the target. Apologize to them for the outburst and then tell them that you yelled at them because you felt they were not acting in their best interest. You can say that you care about them and have their best interest at heart and you are sorry you got so emotional. Tell the person it worries you to think that the person does not have their best interest at heart. On the other hand, you can remind a target when you are criticizing their behavior that you will always be there for them no matter what bad thing another individual does. Ensure that you always ask what you can do to help instead of just criticizing what other people do.

Heal doubt and overcome trust issues.

Individuals who have been manipulated by people before find it hard to trust people and are often on the lookout for this type of behavior, so you have to open your eyes to check for signs. If you think that trust is a problem, the fastest way around that issue is to share a very private and personal thing with the target. It will be better if they feel you have enough trust in them to share something personal with them or if what you share is relevant to them. What is important is that they believe your story and not that it is true. Acting is also key.

When trying to manipulate another individual, the biggest enemy you will have is doubt. They might start getting to see that they are not behaving like themselves if they don't notice anything that is fishy about your behavior. Hopefully, you have learned about some of their problems at this point and found out what they desire to change in their lives. If the way they are acting is openly questioned by them, you need to let them know that change can be uncomfortable but it is necessary to make progress in their lives. Any negativity should be saved for a necessary emotional outburst. When you are trying to convince people to do what you desire, your best friend will always be positivity. The only time to use negative manipulation is when it is necessary as you can become an ineffective manipulator if there is too much negativity.

Step to Take If You Are Discovered.

When many novice manipulators are discovered, they make the mistake of using the tactics discussed above. If your target starts calling you a manipulator, you should not respond with manipulative behavior. This is the worst thing you can do. Be a calm and normal person if you are caught. Allow them to assume control of the situation and don't even try to defend yourself. Once you have been caught, the best way to get out of the situation is to create doubt in your target's mind. Create doubt that is of benefit to you. If your target accuses you of being manipulative and you don't react like one who is manipulative, they will start doubting their thoughts and wonder if they assumed correctly or not. A lot of times, the target will already have an attachment to you and will embrace any excuse to believe they have made a wrong assumption about you. Oftentimes, when someone catches you, it is often because another manipulator or their friend has told them something about you. Be careful, be smart, and be prepared to surprise the person if you suddenly get discovered.

Do you have a friend who seems to follow this manual? Have people been targeting and manipulating you in the past?

Avoiding Techniques Used in Brainwashing

Avoiding techniques used in brainwashing means that you have to avoid the brainwashers themselves, but you know that it can be hard to do this. For example, in advertising, you can't avoid brainwashers, and attempting to avoid them all can be expensive if you still like watching television and movies. The best thing to do is to cut out anything you can and, when it is difficult to cut out, seek balance. It is easy to find balance by simply giving yourself the information you need.

You just need to do the following:

1. Pay attention to the manipulative message that you have received.

2. Look for a message that opposes the manipulative message, whether it is manipulative or not. Try to get the most unbiased and neutral account of that same message.

3. Compare the different sources you have and make a decision about how you feel.

Whether brainwashing is extreme or mild, isolation can make it possible. If the brainwashed message is what you keep hearing regularly, and you don't keep yourself open to alternatives, there is a high probability that you will accept what you hear and not think about it. If you want to avoid the brainwashing techniques we have discussed, you can surround yourself with more information instead of simply accepting the message that you feel comfortable with. After all, that is usually what the message aims to do.

Techniques for Putting Ideas into People's Minds

Some people drive to their deaths in cars wired to bombs. An individual might be told to drive a car with a bomb nearer to a certain people or a place and then detonate it. While one individual may continue thinking about what they have been told and go on to drive the car to their death, another one may stop to think about it and eventually change their mind. Some members of a cult may be brainwashed into drinking poison by their leader. Cult members have committed many ritual suicides.

Brainwashing is powerful. It can convince people to do extreme things and even end their lives. There are many examples of people acting in stupid ways as a result of an idea that was put into their minds. From being convinced to kill innocent people to giving up all the worldly possessions they own, to joining a cult, it appears it is easier to brainwash the human mind than we often like to think.

There are also examples that are not extreme. If you have ever found yourself agreeing to do something you find unpleasant and don't want to do, if you have ever bought a product you didn't really want, or changed an opinion that you had about something after talking to somebody, you have experienced how other people can influence your mind. The mind is like a tablet that can be easily written upon and shaped by others. Have you always wondered what you can do to brainwash people?

Many people are fascinated with techniques to put ideas into the minds of individuals. Having the skill to enter into the dreams of people to learn their secrets could be something desirable. If there is any skill like this and you have it, you can enter someone's dream to plant an idea. The assumption is that an individual's mind can be changed from within, making them believe that the idea was their own idea.

You might be saying to yourself, "I can't enter people's dreams." You can still plant ideas in people's minds and get what you want without entering their dreams. These brainwashing techniques have the power to be destructive. Ensure that you use the techniques to brainwash individuals ethically and responsibly. Positive brainwashing has the power to make your relationships better and impress people at events.

What if you had the skills to plant ideas in the minds of people? Imagine what you could do with that. You might use it to get a date, a large sum of money, or a job. You could easily bring awkward disagreements to an end if you were able to plant an idea inside an individual's mind, while the individual believes that they actually thought of the idea themselves. So, how can you put an idea into a person's mind? We will discuss that.

Embedded Commands and Word Ambiguity to Put Ideas into People's Minds

You might hear the sentence, "You must have made up your mind by now," and it may appear innocent until you discover that the command "by now" is contained in it. Salespeople and therapists often use this method of embedding commands in seemingly innocuous sentences.

Suppose you are trying to win over someone you like and want to date. "You love gadgets like me." This sentence contains "like me" which is the embedded command, and emphasizing certain words can have the effect of highlighting your message that is hidden, e.g. "I don't know what you want to do, but I will be going out, if you would like to go with me."

In essence, these techniques are reliant on clever wordplay. If you have ever misheard the lyrics of a song or fallen for a joke, you will know that there can be a misinterpretation of certain phrases. When you use ambiguity in your speech, you are subtly conveying a message without saying what you are saying directly. There are a variety of ambiguous sentences that you can use.

Hypnotists and practitioners of NLP usually change the way their patients think by pronouncing sentences in ambiguous ways. Look for any combination of words that you could put a hidden message into. The words should sound similar, and the hidden message can be in a seemingly innocent sentence. An innocent thing you say could bring another idea into the individual's mind.

Priming.

Priming, which is often used by hypnotists is when an idea is suggested at the level that the other individual is not consciously aware of. If you provide a list of the words "rabbit," "chicken, and "dog," and ask a person to tell you one word that has the same rhyme as "hat," they will most likely say the word "cat" because they have a mind that is primed to think of animals.

Some people fool their participants into thinking that they telepathically guess which item their participants think of when they have primed their participants to think of a particular item.

Priming is also commonly used in advertising. Studies show that the amount of food people eat on a particular day can be increased with exposure to food advertisements. Marketing companies prime us to spend, and it is evident in all the images and messages we receive every day. When individuals are asked to recite the Ten Commandments before performing a task, the likelihood of cheating will be low, and when people are exposed to messages that have to do with old age, it can make people walk more slowly. Making an individual think along certain lines is capable of influencing the decisions the individual makes later.

Here is one trick you can try: prime the mind of your participant to think of red items. This can be done by pointing out a red thing, putting on a red shirt, or humming the tune to a song with red as the hook. You can do this creatively. Make sure that the tactics you use are not too obvious. Some minutes later, you can tell another friend involved in the conversation that you will be able to make a guess about what fruit your primed friend will mention. You can then ask your primed friend to mention the name of the first fruit that is on their mind. Because of the red priming, they will likely think and then say "apple".

Prime a person into being more agreeable by starting a conversation with questions that generate many "yes" responses. "It is a beautiful weather today, isn't it?" and some other questions that are yes-inducing can increase an individual's likelihood to say yes to suggestions you make.

If the idea you want to plant involves money, for instance, you want to get an increase in salary, priming the person for kindness and empathy is better, as people are less inclined to share their wealth when they think about money. The most effective way to go about this is to make them think about their pride in their own generosity and their social connections by asking them about their hobbies or family.

Brainwashing by Being Incomplete.

An individual might reject an idea if you offer it to them directly. Many people like to know that they are clever and that they thought of an idea on their own. We often reject ideas that other people offer us and cling to our own ideas. The trick here is to convince the individual that the idea you have is actually their own idea. This technique is common in sales and advertising. When an advert uses images of beautiful women wearing perfume, it does not mean that buying and using the perfume will make you look beautiful, but your brain has to put the pieces together.

If you want to plant an idea in a person's mind and make them believe the idea was actually their own idea, you can lay clues without making it obvious. You need to be patient when doing this because impatience will ruin everything. This doesn't need to be rushed, but it should be done over time.

If you and your partner are looking for holiday destinations and your partner prefers Europe for the holiday, while you have been dreaming of Hawaii, you could tell your partner about a crime that has happened in Europe and ensure that you talk about it occasionally or talk about how expensive things are there. You can then promote your preferred destination without making it too obvious.

One thing you can do is to play dumb. You can suggest to your partner that it would be nice if you could go somewhere that has great cocktails and beaches. If you effectively include things available in Hawaii in your suggestion without making it obvious, your partner might decide that Hawaii should be the place for the holiday.

Once your partner starts thinking they are smart for bringing up the right destination, they will see it as their idea. They will form an attachment to the idea. You can also leave a beach picture lying around as this will create extra effect. This might not be consciously noticed by them, but the beach's picture will linger in their mind.

You can pretend that someone previously told you something. In this case, you can say something like, "I'm sure you are the one who told me…" or "You were saying that…" Even if the person can't remember saying this to you, a positive statement you attribute to them can make them claim it. Many individuals start believing they must have said it and then feel pride over the idea and claim ownership.

This method will be effective for giving advice. If a friend of yours finds it difficult to take advice, you may avoid giving them instructions and still tell them what to do. You can ask them leading questions. If you notice that they need to ask for an increase in salary at work, you could ask them if they have thought about what they need to do to make more money.

They will then think about a pay raise as the solution and you will smile and congratulate them on thinking about that idea. This technique is often used by therapists to make their clients feel in control of their lives. It gives their clients a feeling of power. This technique is effective as no one likes the feeling of being told what to do.

Using Reverse Psychology

If you consider yourself someone who is a rebel, there is a probability that you don't like people telling you what to do. Instead of asking someone to tidy their room, and you tell them that you bet they couldn't keep their room clean even if they tried, don't you think they will be moved to tidy their room? People are wise these days and you can't just tell them the opposite of something you want them to do and expect them to do what you want. You can't just say, "Don't buy me a gift, then," when you actually want them to buy you a gift.

Reverse psychology is often used in advertising. If you have ever fallen in love with a product because it was limited or expensive, this technique might have been responsible for it. People don't often care much about what they can easily get; they seem to desire what is hard to get.

This is also used in dating. Once a woman has become attracted to you, you might say, "This would never work between us. I have to stop this now." You might also start acting as if you are not interested in a relationship with her. A woman who is used to always getting what she wants will start seeing you as a very interesting person and they will be convinced that you are the one they want to be with. Reverse psychology is considered more passive-aggressive than when an idea is planted into the mind.

Reverse psychology is usually more effective on argumentative or rebellious people. When you say something like, "The roller coaster is too scary; I don't think you would like it," it can make your friend get a ride ticket. They will want to try the ride because of your bold statement. Your friend will start wondering what you know about them and this can convince them to try the ride. Your friend will be thinking, "What do they know about me?" and this convinces your friend that trying the thing you suggested that they avoid was their own idea. Be careful when you use this technique. You don't use it for everything. For example, if you tell your friend not to date a girl, they might believe your words and stay single.

Although we are manipulated daily by politicians, advertisers, and others, the idea of manipulating someone's mind is ethically questionable. Manipulation from politicians might be in subtle form, where the politician says something that makes you feel good and you then conclude his other statements must also be good. Once something is expensive, you might conclude that it must be good.

Brainwashing can be used to improve your life and it can also be used for evil. You can use it to make things flow smoothly for you without hurting anybody in the process. It can improve situations and make the world we live in a better place. Imagine using brainwashing to make more people care for the environment, to be kind to each other, or to eat more healthy meals. When you use techniques of brainwashing properly, it opens up doors that you may have considered impossible. If you don't want to use brainwashing techniques, you don't have to.

How to Avoid Manipulation

Accept thoughts, fears, and pain.
You will experience unpleasant feelings as you heal from brainwashing. You need to deprogram your mind and get out of your manipulator's world. When you accept the manipulator's plans and how they mask themselves with a nice face to try to harm you, you will experience one of the most rational and irrational emotions, which is fear. A therapist or good domestic attorney for violence can help you overcome your fears in a productive and healthy manner.

Gain knowledge about different kinds of abuse.
There is power in knowledge, and you can use it to successfully stop your manipulator's attempts to degrade and humiliate you. The probability of feeling worse about the words and actions of your manipulator will be low when you know your abuser harms you because they want to control you. Learn and understand as much as possible what you need to know about domestic violence and abuse. With time, you will know how to recognize the kinds of verbal abuse your partner makes you experience. When you understand the different types of abuse and you can identify them, you will be able to detach from harmful words and behaviors as you will know when

your manipulator is trying to cause you harm. Be aware of what type of abuse is out there, and how the abuse looks and sounds, and note the feelings the abuse gives you. One question you might have asked yourself is why does the abuser abuse you? Do not spend too much time trying to research the answer.

Put an end to isolation.

One fast way to get over any fear that you have is opening up about your feelings and the situation. It is wise to discuss the manipulation with a therapist. You may not be ready to talk about this, but you can start by talking about last night's football match or talking about the weather, as you will gain some confidence with this. When you isolate yourself, it doesn't completely make brainwashing end. Surround yourself with individuals who are aware of your abuse and who can give you their support.

Dealing with fear and anxiety.

Leaving the manipulator is an appropriate stress reliever for individuals who have experienced manipulation. That way, the victim will experience peace in a way that they have never imagined they would experience. Many individuals are not ready to quit, and they may choose to remain with the manipulator forever. You can handle stress and anxiety by having proper nutrition, practicing hypnosis if you are a victim of abuse, getting proper medical care, listening to music, practicing meditation techniques, practicing breathing techniques, and taking a walk during your spare time.

Manipulation and Force

At least, psychological and social force is incorporated in every case of manipulation; it doesn't involve physical force. You also need to know that there is a difference between brainwashing and manipulation. In brainwashing, the individual is aware that the aggressor is an enemy. During wars, the belief system of prisoners was changed through the use of brainwashing. Physical force is involved in brainwashing, and the individual concerned is made to do what they would normally not do. However, the brainwashing effects disappear when they escape the enemy.

This aspect increases mind manipulation's effectiveness and makes it more dangerous than abuse, torture, physical coercion, and brainwashing. Remember that physical coercion is not involved in mind manipulation, but it has a higher effectiveness than other techniques. Although brainwashing can change an individual's behavior, mind manipulation can change the person's entire beliefs, thinking processes, attitudes, behaviors, and personality. Also, the individual will happily and actively take part in the change process, because they believe that it is the best thing to do.

It is difficult to believe that you were actually being manipulated by someone you liked, trusted, and helped. That is something that makes it difficult to help an individual in a manipulative relationship. They find it hard to believe that they are being manipulated by the manipulator. The victim will find it hard to let go of the changes that had taken place even when they are free from the manipulator's grip. When we are pushed to make decisions, the effect doesn't last as long as when we make decisions for ourselves. It is difficult to admit that an individual who is close to us was responsible for certain decisions we made.

Ensure that you don't harm other people or ignore their desires even though you have learned how to use manipulation to achieve your desires. Manipulation will involve persuasion, coaxing, charm, and maybe some trickery and misdirection. You shouldn't be using manipulation to make everyone give you what you desire regardless of the negative consequences that may be involved. Manipulation should be done in such a way that you get what you want and also leave the other individual better than you met them.

Your desires are not the only important issues, so you need to use manipulation in such a way that you do not hurt other people.

Understand that those around you have needs that might match with your needs and you can find a situation that is a win for all involved. People will easily trust you if they feel that their needs matter and they don't feel manipulated.

CHAPTER SIX:
Dark Psychology Red Flags

There are red flags of dark psychology that you need to know about. This is necessary to understand it fully. Once you have this knowledge, you can use it when you want and you can also protect yourself from the manipulation and influence of others.

Let us take a look at some common dark psychology red flags:

Isolate victims from family and friends.
People using dark psychology on others may try to isolate the individuals from their family and friends to be able to exert more control over them and influence their actions.

Acting too nice, shallow flattery, and superficial compliments.
The most charming and nicest girl or guy in the room is usually looked at suspiciously by therapists. This is often the case because they are usually putting on a show and on the high side of acceptable narcissism. They are hiding their true personality and not showing it. You need to be careful because they may do it in a humble way which makes it hard to notice or they may do it in a flashy attention-seeking manner. If a person is always flattering you, giving you compliments, and being so sweet and nice to you, that person is probably too good to be true. When people want to hook you in and then manipulate you and disappoint you later, they usually display this behavior. At the beginning of a relationship, if a person behaves more like your butler than actually acting like your girlfriend or boyfriend that they are, this person may have attachment or boundary issues. Look for nice romantic partners and friends but if it

appears phony, over the top, or not genuine, then you need to pay attention.

Pressure people to make fast decisions.
People using dark psychology on others may try to pressure these individuals into making fast decisions, thereby giving the individuals little or no time to reflect on the request and consider it.

Intimidation tactics.
People controlling others through dark psychology may use intimidation tactics to control their victims and influence their behavior.

Making victims feel ashamed or guilty.
People may use dark psychology to try to manipulate individuals by making them feel ashamed or guilty.

Flatter people excessively.
People who use dark psychology may gain other people's trust and influence over them by flattering them excessively. Flattery exploits people's healthy and normal need to build authentic connections with other people. Social interactions may use flattery as a tactic in which the flatterer desires to gain something from the person they are flattering. This tactic of coercion is quite effective. When someone flatters you, they make you feel better about yourself, which makes you start seeing them in a more positive way. This increases the likelihood of you complying with the plan they have for you. Potential voters may be flattered by politicians. Employees may be flattered by their employers to give them an artificial morale boost and increase their productivity. Clergy might get tithes from their congregation by flattering them. When a leader is criticized, they might use flattery to disarm their critics and shame them. A sexual predator might groom a person they are targeting by using flattery.

The flattery is usually directed at something that the recipient considers important to them and it is done in a way that doesn't appear obvious enough for it to be confronted or pointed out.

How Flattery Manipulates an Individual's Emotions

Flattery is capable of creating a false sense of admiration and trust, which can make an individual more open to other forms of manipulation. It has the ability to make a person feel important and special, which can lower the person's defenses and make them more open to the requests of the manipulator.

Flattery has the ability to manipulate people's emotions, thereby clouding their judgment and making them feel good about themselves. This can make it hard for a person to see the true motives of the manipulator and recognize that the manipulator is manipulating them. A sense of loyalty or obligation is created, and this can make a person feel like they need to do what the manipulator is asking them to do in order for the manipulator to maintain the positive opinion they have about them or in order that they will not let the manipulator down.

The manipulator can also use flattery to distract their target from their true intentions, making the target look away from their actions' negative consequences and focus on the positive feedback they are getting. This makes the target depend on the approval and validation of the manipulator, making the target rely more on them and then do whatever they ask them to do.

Combination of Manipulation and Flattery

Flattery may appear appealing and enjoyable at first, just like a sweet candy. But too much of it can be harmful to you.

In the same way that consuming too much candy can cause tooth decay and weight gain, too much flattery can make an individual lack critical thinking and have a distorted sense of reality.

Just like candy is meant to be enjoyed in moderation, ensure that you are wary of too much flattery and be aware that it can deceive and manipulate people. Manipulation can be likened to when the strings of the puppet are being pulled by the puppet master. Being in control, the puppet master, who is the manipulator, has the ability to make the victim do whatever they want them to do, but the victim has no idea that they are being manipulated and may think that their decisions are being made by them.

Manipulation involves influencing or controlling an individual in a deceptive way, causing them to do things that they may not have considered doing if they were not manipulated. In the same way that a puppet does not know anything about the manipulation, an individual being manipulated may have no idea of the manipulator's true motives. But when flattery is combined with manipulation, it is a dangerous mix because when they are combined, they work well at controlling and influencing people. The individual may not even know that the manipulator is manipulating them, and this is what makes this type of manipulation harmful.

The individual may be doing whatever the manipulator asks them to do out of loyalty and love because they think that the manipulator actually has their best interests at heart.

This makes it hard for the individual to recognize what is happening and resist the manipulation, and the individual may end up doing things that are harmful to them and not in their own best interest.

Flattery can be used to manipulate people in the following contexts:

A salesperson's flattery: A salesman or woman can use flattery to make you buy a product you don't need.

Flattering a partner in a relationship: When a partner constantly dishes compliments to the other partner, they may be doing their best to manipulate or control them.

Flattery from family members: A family member may be trying to manipulate you into doing something that is in their own interest by constantly giving you compliments.

Flattery from friends: If you have a friend who always compliments you, they may be trying to get you to do something that is in their own interest that you don't want to do.

Flattery on social media: A social media user may use flattery to get close to you. They may constantly comment on your posts or like your posts because they are trying to gain your trust or attention.

Flattering colleagues at work: You may have a boss who always praises you at work. This person may be praising you because they want you to do something that will benefit them and not you.

Flattery in dating: An individual may try to win your affection by using flattery to manipulate you into going deeper into the relationship than you would like.

Flattery deceives an individual while praise offers encouragement. When someone flatters another person, they hope to get something done without thinking about the individual who receives the flattery. The flatterer usually has an ulterior motive that is beneficial to them alone. Praise, on the other hand, is beneficial to the person receiving it as it encourages the person being praised to see the positive aspects of life. Praise makes it possible for others to recognize the talents they have, increase their self-esteem, give direction, and restore hope. It is helpful to both the receiver and the giver.

CHAPTER SEVEN:
Dark Psychology in Relationships

An individual in a relationship can fulfill their own needs by using the techniques of dark psychology at the expense of their partner.

Can you make someone open up and connect deeply with them? To answer this question easily, you need to think back to how often and when somebody said any of the following to you, "you are the only person I can really discuss this issue with," "You are the only person who truly understands what I am talking about," "you are the first individual I have ever talked to about this." If people usually say this kind of stuff to you regularly, it means you definitely know how to get other people to open up to you and you know how to connect with them on a deeper level. The answers show that somebody found you to be a confidant. You are a person they can trust and be open, honest, and vulnerable with.

If you have heard these sentences several times in your life from people who are close to you and even strangers you are just getting to know, it means that you have the ability to connect with people easily and on a deeper level. You may be thinking that your connection with people is just a mere coincidence and you just happened to be in the right place at the right time. The lifeblood of all relationships that are important is your ability to connect deeply with other individuals. If you examine your connections and relations to see how they started, you can make a conscious effort to increase the level of your interactions. Examining your connections and relationships will reveal to you that most individuals have "shadow" parts that they hide and only reveal to a few individuals. You can make a true connection with someone if you can find your way to these shadow parts they have, and you can do this by accepting the person for who they really are. When you analyze the most vulnerable moments that you have shared with others, you will discover that these moments of opening up, vulnerability, and connection did not just happen by random coincidence.

Making A Person Fall in Love with You

Have you ever been drawn to an individual whose presence brings you warmth and also sudden coldness? The person comes close to you and then retreats, and this pattern leaves you wanting more of them. This relationship is not just a troubled one; the person is deliberate with this tactic. This dark manipulation technique switches between pleasure and pain.

The person lures you in with affection and then comes the sting of their absence. Isn't this confusing? One day, you are showered with so much attention, and the next day, you are left alone in the cold, wondering if you are even worth anything to that person. This dark manipulation technique thrives on this kind of confusion. The cycle continues. There is a period where affection is intense and then after that comes a sudden withdrawal of affection, where the warmth disappears. You become addicted to this push-and-pull game where you don't know what the rules are and your emotional well-being is at risk.

Everyone is a manipulator, at least to an extent. Connections are fostered through the use of social cues like eye contact and smiles. But when someone is using manipulation to control someone to their own advantage and not to form a connection, a line is crossed. This is not a healthy interaction. The strategy is used to make a person dependent on the manipulator to give them emotional validation.

There is a price associated with a manipulated heart. Such manipulation has a steep cost. The manipulated person usually experiences a plummeting self-esteem, and they also experience depression and anxiety. There is a relentless pursuit of approval, which binds the person tighter to the manipulator, who is the source of the person's pain. This dependency is harmful, and the cycle feeds on the victim's need for validation.

Let us discuss some dark psychological tactics that you can use to make someone fall in love with you.

Select the victim that is suitable, you need to choose the suitable person because you can't pick someone who has high self-esteem and is happy with their life. The person has to have a need in their life that has not been met. To get the person to fall in love with you, you need to find their place of vulnerability and then provide validation for the person's vulnerability.

Send the person mixed signals to make them believe that they have your heart and then withdraw from them. The person has to feel the loss of losing you and you have to make that happen.

You need to have qualities that are contrasting. For instance, if there is a woman you like and want to make her fall in love with you, having an air of femininity to strike a balance is important. A person who is too masculine shows insecurity because over-masculinity shows over-compensation. When you strike a balance, you appear more trustworthy.

Talk about other women as this will help you create a triangle of desire. The female you talk about should have a look that is opposite to how she looks. When you let her know the type of women you find attractive, it creates competition. This can inflict pain, and you don't have to be afraid of doing this. You have the power to also inflict pleasure if you can inflict pain.

Plant insecurities in her and do it at a subconscious level. You can do this by talking about something you are aware will be difficult for her to meet, mentioning it while having a conversation with her, and then changing the topic quickly. Don't give her time to elaborate on the topic you mentioned. You just need to plant the seed in the woman's subconscious mind.

Set up barriers and challenges. Interaction becomes a lot better when you set intentional challenges. Create temptation that will bring the relationship to life and enjoy teasing her. Women usually appreciate men who tease them. They will feel frustrated, and this frustration increases their desire for you.

Giving the woman thoughtful gifts helps. Pay attention to them and find out what they love. You can then give them a unique gift. When you give them gifts, it makes them believe that they are on your mind. During the relationship, you can take a step back and then return.

Disarm the woman with vulnerability. When you show vulnerability, the woman is able to see the real human in you.

Be unable to control yourself when you are around her, showing her that you find it hard to resist her charm and she is too beautiful. People enjoy being admired by others so this could be a flattering situation for them. It also helps you to hide these tactics.

Give the woman space because she will fall in love with you when you are not around her. When you back off a bit, it allows her to think of you, and her view of you is also enhanced.

Engage in the woman's deepest narcissism. If you embody the idealized person that she is, she will love you. Don't give her room to take you for granted. Ensure that you use pleasure, pain, and absence as it will make her appreciate you.

Find the woman's secret fantasy and make it a reality. If you can do this, you will see that she will become obsessed with you. She experiences your power and also experiences you when she feels your boundaries, so ensure that she feels your boundaries.

The more subtle your mixed signals and your disinterest the better things will work. You have to make the woman not know you, but make her interpret you.

Techniques of Dark Psychology in Dating

1. Wearing a mask.

This dark psychology technique is when someone wears a mask of the ideal partner, thereby pretending to have the same goals and interests as a person with the aim of advancing the relationship. For instance, a person might pretend to share similar interests and hobbies with you or love those hobbies and interests when they actually don't like them.

Strategy for avoidance: Maintain your interests and individuality in a relationship. If an individual appears to be too eager to align with your preferences, ensure that you are cautious about that. Create room for open discussions about differences as this will contribute to establish a genuine connection.

2. Pretending to have low interest.

Female dark psychologists stay in control of their relationship by pretending to have low interest in their partner. This makes them appear as a prize, thereby manipulating the man to continue chasing them. The lady might pretend that she is not interested in the relationship when she is really interested.

Strategy for avoidance: Understand the value of interest and mutual respect in a relationship. Avoid chasing an individual who keeps playing hard to get. There has to be equal investment from both parties to have a healthy relationship.

3. False commitment.

A man may use dark psychology to deceive a lady by pretending that they are interested in having a committed relationship while lying to them and giving them false promises. The man might make the lady believe that he wants to have a future with her but avoid making an actual commitment to the relationship.

Strategy for avoidance: An individual should ensure that they make honest and open communication a priority in their relationship. They should see that actions and words align over time. They should also pay attention and notice any discrepancies that may occur between a person's actual behavior and their stated intentions. Expectations and long-term goals should be discussed early in the relationship.

4. Using sex as a reward or punishment.

Some people use sex as a punishment or reward to achieve what they want in their relationship. For example, they might control their partner by withholding intimacy from them.

Strategy for avoidance: Ensure that intimacy is not used as a bargaining chip in a relationship. Intimacy should be based on consent and mutual desire. Be open about communication and talk about boundaries and expectations concerning physical intimacy.

CHAPTER EIGHT:
Dark Psychology in Business and Groups

Dark psychology is capable of manipulating employees in the workplace into ignoring their own interests and prioritizing the interests of the company.

Techniques of Dark Psychology in Business

1. Dark leadership personality traits.

Some organizations are good at unintentionally encouraging dark personality traits in the organization's managers, thereby making the work environment toxic. When choosing employers, employees need to be cautious and avoid depending on superiors for support. For example, a company's manager might manipulate the workers into doing more work without adequate compensation for the extra time worked by putting emphasis on how important it is for the company to be successful.

Strategy of avoidance: Check for the leadership qualities that potential managers possess when you are choosing an employer. Stay away from organizations that promote toxic work environments. Be an advocate for proper compensation and fair treatment in your place of work.

2. Corporate manipulation.

A company may guilt-trip employees into accepting unfavorable conditions for the company's greater good. Slogans such as "we are a family" and "employees matter," are used by companies to guilt-trip employees and make them care more about the company's benefit than their personal well-being.

Strategy for avoidance: Pay attention to corporate messages and slogans that promote sacrificing oneself for the organization. Make your rights as an employee and your well-being a priority. Seek fairness and transparency in the organization's policies.

The impact of dark psychology is undeniably far-reaching and profound even though it may not hold an official designation in the realm of psychology. This discipline involves using psychological tactics to accomplish sinister ends. When you understand these techniques, you will be able to recognize when you are being manipulated and then protect yourself from the effects. Staying vigilant and informed in the face of potential manipulation is important.

Understanding Sales Psychology

Salespeople use sales psychology to make their prospective customers feel good about themselves. People remember more the feelings you made them experience than what you say to them. This means that customers remember more of how you make them feel. Therefore, tactics that are very powerful in sales are the ones that make customers feel really good about themselves, and these tactics include psychological ones. Sales psychology has the ability to make prospects feel good about themselves. It helps salesmen and saleswomen close deals.

Things go deeper than simply feeling good, even though it is at the core of sales psychology. Why salespeople use psychological tactics explains how they use the tactics in their sales strategy.

Using Psychology in Sales

When psychology in sales is involved, the reason salespeople use it explains how they use it. Making customers feel really good about themselves is at the core of why successful salesmen and saleswomen use psychology.

But, you don't really get the whole story from that, as you could also make someone feel good in many other ways. Sales reps sometimes feel like they are being manipulative or malicious by using sales psychology. Because prospects have a short attention span and many of them would get lost during the sales process, sales reps use psychology. It is not just prospects that have a short attention span; humans in general do. This is why sales psychology is used.

If they didn't use sales psychology, it would be hard to get prospects to focus and not get lost during the sales process. If they don't use psychology, prospects would not focus on the solution in front of them and would struggle to make the right decision that would help them.

Let us look at the how. Salespeople use psychology to convince prospects to make a particular decision. With sales psychology, the salespeople tap into the brains of their prospects to influence their decisions. If you are a salesperson, don't ever feel bad about swaying prospect decision-making by using psychological tactics. All you are doing is to help them see that you have the right solution for them, and this makes them feel amazing.

A difference exists between low-pressure selling and high-pressure selling. Most people do not enjoy feeling like someone is selling something to them. For instance, do you enjoy getting the sense that the salesperson doesn't care a bit about you and is only selling to you in their own interest? Most people dislike being sold to.

Part of high-pressure selling is the feeling that you are being sold to. It involves the feeling that someone is making you make a decision to buy. And this experience is not a positive sales experience. Low-pressure selling is the opposite kind of approach. Prospects feel good with the psychological tactics it uses, and when prospects feel good, more deals are closed.

Moreover, these tactics are within the approach of low-pressure selling. People who are the best at sales do their best to make their prospects feel good. They do this because they know that someone is empowered and they are close to closing a deal when the customer feels good.

When sales psychology tactics are used in a low-pressure sales approach, it leads to a win for salespeople and prospects.

1. Techniques of sales psychology used for lead generation.

There is probably nothing better in sales than when leads come to you, instead of creating the list yourself. Lead generation, which is the first stage of the sales process, can be started with sales psychology.

You can begin to fill your sales funnel with leads by allowing them to come to you. Before you even reach out, you can even warm them up to the person that you are.

These two sales tactics knock lead generation out of the park by using psychology.

Mirror the identity of your lead.

People naturally gravitate towards those people who they feel are like them. Most especially, individuals who they believe think like them, act like them or have the same values as them.

Although it is a little unnerving to realize that people unconsciously gravitate towards what they consider similar, this fact can be used to your advantage in sales.

Work with your marketing team to release content that reflects some aspect of your ideal lead.

For instance, if you have ideal leads with a social media profile that shows how committed they are, you can do the same thing in your own content. It doesn't mean that you should do a full sustainability campaign, but you can even make a few posts that will do the trick if it shows your similarity.

This will then make your lead recognize that you and them are similar, and it will make them more likely to reach out. And even if you are the one who makes the first move, the likelihood of them responding will increase.

Show potential leads your social proof.

I'm sure you know what peer pressure is. It doesn't suddenly end after high school. You can get leads into the sales funnel by using a modified version of peer pressure, and this is a sales psychology tactic that is very effective. This is called "pressure" in life and called "social proof" in sales.

Social proof allows potential leads to see that others are taking advantage of the solution your business is providing and they are reaping the benefits.

For instance, you can make a post on your social media platforms talking about how the lives of your current customers have become better after working with you. This will make your potential leads believe that it will work for them if it actually works for those people. And then a new lead will enter your sales funnel. Although some people think that social proof is a manipulative, misleading, and negative tactic, this is not the case.

If you believe you have a solution that is excellent and has the ability to solve the challenges that people have, what is preventing you from getting the solution into their hands?

There is no harm if you need to use social proof to make leads see that you can solve their problems.

2. Techniques of sales psychology for outreach.

After filling your pipeline with leads, you can reach out to them directly and turn them into prospects.

Whether this is the first time you are connecting with them, or they showed interest in you themselves, sales psychology can be used by you to your advantage.

Salespeople can use the following two psychological techniques during the sales process' outreach stage.

Expectations should be uprooted.

Are you aware that your brain is constantly trying to work ahead of you? Are you aware that it tries to predict what is about to come next in a sequence and you don't even know it?

Your brain will be a bit taken aback when it sees something other than what it wanted to see in a particular sentence.

This think-ahead strategy of the brain can be used by sales reps to their advantage. You can do it this way:

Try to flip your language when you are writing a sales cold email. Instead of saying what the prospect would expect you to say, uproot what they expect you to say. When the expectations of the brain are uprooted, the brain remembers it for a long time. Uprooting expectations helps you stay memorable. When you are memorable, it is also a sales psychology tactic. The prospect will see you as an authority in their domain when you are memorable.

Reciprocity.

Imagine this scenario: You have the perfect cold-calling script as well as your ideal leads. You manage to put in some sentences after the lead answers the phone. But the line then goes dead all of a sudden.

What is the best way to cold-call leads and get them to listen and not hang up the phone? Sales psychology can do the trick.

If you are making cold calls to your prospects and taking some of their time, you should have a valuable thing to give them in return.

For instance, you can inform the prospect that you ran an analysis on their company and you discovered a problem that you want to discuss with them. You are offering them value when you do this. Reciprocity is then initiated.

The reciprocity concept entails that someone will naturally want to give you something in return when you give them something valuable. So, if you show the prospects something valuable or hidden about their company that they are not aware of, the prospects will set up a formal sales meeting to reciprocate your generosity.

Remember, don't wish to get something for nothing. You need to offer the prospects something that they will consider valuable when you cold call to make them reciprocate the favor.

3. Techniques of sales psychology for qualifying.

At this point, you have reached out to leads and made them agree to a sales call. Great. As you qualify these leads as a fit for your solution, ensure that you keep the psychological momentum going. Keep in mind that this stage's goal is to find out the pain points of the prospects and then begin to build rapport. Successful salesmen and saleswomen use these psychological tactics to do both of those things:

The fear of missing out.

The fear of missing out or FOMO is a term that has been made popular by social media. It is a feeling that people get when they think that they will lose out on a positive thing if they fail to purchase a particular product or service.

For instance, a company selling sales services can make you feel that you are missing out when you don't buy from them, and they can use tactics to make you feel this way. So, you will want to buy from them because you believe you will have a perfectly organized sales process.

It is not too early to start creating a sense of FOMO even though you are still in the process of qualifying the prospect. A highly effective tactic is sharing a case study as it will make the prospects feel some fear of missing out.

You can share a case study with them when you get to the end of your initial sales call, as it will help to create a sense of FOMO inside the prospects. This will increase their readiness to move ahead into the sales process' next stage.

Make the prospects feel in control.

You need to ask the prospects the right questions if you want to know their pain points.

However, when you ask questions, it creates a negative side effect where the prospect feels like they have no control at all over the situation. This can make them leave.

What if you can get the information you need from the prospects without asking them questions? The good news is, you can. These negotiation tactics can make the prospect talk about their problems and you don't have to ask them any questions before they talk about the problems. The effect is the same as questioning. This way, they feel like they are in control of the situation and you also get the information you need.

Prospects' self-esteem increases when you make them feel in control. They will not feel trampled by you but will feel empowered by you.

4. Techniques of sales psychology for the sales pitch.

Lastly, you are at the sales pitch. Unless you have a sales cycle that is very drawn out, this is the final step before the buying decision is made.

You can use the pitch as the time to shine. If you still feel like you haven't convinced the prospect enough, this is the time to let them see all the value your solution will bring them. When you are making sales pitches, you can use sales psychology to show the prospects that you are capable of turning all the issues they have into strengths.

Dress and look the part.

Although this one is quite obvious, don't forget to dress as the individual you want to be when you show up to your sales pitches. And this person, hopefully, is a salesperson that is successful. Ensure that you show up as if you are a successful salesperson even if you don't believe in yourself at the moment.

When you dress the part of a salesperson that is successful, an additional layer of storytelling is added to your pitch. You also feel like you are at your very best. This will help you emit positive energy when you feel great about yourself, and your prospects will also feel a positive energy. The prospects embrace your pitch even more when they feel the positive energy.

Dressing the part makes you feel good about yourself, and the aura of the sales pitch is changed for the better.

Use the customer's needs to create a storyline.
What makes individuals purchase the things that they purchase?

People usually purchase products or services that match their internal narrative. A narrative can be referred to as a story.

Stories help with sales, and it is left for you to create a story out of your prospect's problems when making the sales pitch. While your prospects should be the superhero in the story, your solution should be what magically saves the day.

Prospects' emotional desires are satisfied by stories. And this is responsible for their purchasing decision. You should be thinking big if you desire to create a storyline that is effective. If you want to make your pitches into a story that your prospects will find hard to resist, here is how to do it. Although this might sound crazy in the beginning, your sales will sink if you fail to create a storyline that is effective.

5. Techniques of sales psychology for closing the deal.
Although the sales pitch might seem like the process has come to an end, you might still lose the sale when you try to lay the deal on the table. This stage of closing the deal is usually the most difficult. But,

you can still change things. Using the following sales psychology tactics at the end of the process will help you stay in control of the situation until the end.

Reduce the number of available options.

Have you ever walked into an ice cream store, only to find many flavors that blew you away? The store has every kind of flavor, including even the ones you have never seen.

You suddenly discover that you have been at the counter for more than ten minutes without making a decision. You are not the only one getting frustrated, but those standing behind you are also getting frustrated.

Although your business may not be an ice cream store, your prospects can also experience something similar if the options you give them are too many. It will overwhelm them and they will not have a good experience.

Whether you believe this or not, the likelihood of abandoning a situation or having a negative experience increases when you have more options. So, ensure that you don't confuse your prospects with too many options to select from when you lay your deal down on the table. Giving them about 3 options is okay. You are not helping them by giving them more options, but the opposite is actually the case. You can give them 3 choices so they don't begin to develop negative feelings right before you close the sale.

Create time that is limited.

So, you have laid your offer on the table, but your prospects are not forthcoming, but they are hesitating. A long silence starts to fill the room. Your prospects are not screaming yes to your offer as you thought they would. Instead, they are contemplating what decision to take. Although you have done your best right up until this point, you are beginning to feel that you are losing the sale.

To stop this from happening to you, ensure that you create a sense of urgency when you discuss the deal's terms. Creating a sense of urgency means that you should make your prospects feel like they will lose out on something valuable if they delay accepting your offer.

An effective way to do this is to give them a unique offer, in which you include something extra in their deal if they are willing to accept the offer right away.

When you offer your prospects a special thing for only a limited time, it will make them quickly say yes to the deal.

You need to know how to work with people if you want to be successful in business. It will be difficult for you to be successful in sales if you can't work well with people.

Dark Psychology in Groups

Dark psychology is used in group settings, where the group leaders aim to increase their influence and control over the members of the group. Let us take a look at some examples of how the techniques of dark psychology can manifest in groups:

1. Fabricating an external threat.
A leader of a group may try to unify the group by fabricating a common external threat. This will create cohesion among the group members and also create a sense of protection. The group leader might make an imaginary enemy that the group can only defeat.

Strategy for avoidance: Pay attention to attempts to create an external enemy and be critical of it. Check whether the perceived threat is actually exaggerated to manipulate people or if it is real. Encourage unity and cooperation based on shared values and not threats that were manufactured.

2. Dismissing dissenting opinions.
Group leaders may dismiss or discredit dissenting opinions that

abound within the group, thereby ensuring the group members stay loyal to the beliefs and commands of the group. This may include labeling dissenters as outsiders or traitors.

Strategy for avoidance: Create room for an inclusive and open environment where you embrace diverse opinions. Pay attention to groups that stop dissenting voices because it can result in groupthink. Encourage constructive criticism and healthy debate.

3. Exaggerating the severity of problems.
Leaders of groups often exaggerate the severity of issues, thereby convincing the group members that it will be difficult to solve the problems on their own and that they need the guidance of the group to solve the issues. This then increases the group members' dependency on the group leader. For example, the leader of a cult might inflate the perceived threats that their followers are receiving to their well-being.

Strategy of avoidance: Ensure that you pay attention and ask questions when you find yourself facing exaggerated problems. Look at different perspectives and verify them independently before accepting an issue's severity. Avoid making hasty decisions borne from inflated concerns.

CONCLUSION

After reading this book, understanding people's thoughts and how to change them will no longer be a problem for you. We have talked about how you can use dark psychology to do this.

Dark psychology is a common technique many individuals and companies use to influence lives daily. Politicians use it to convince people and get what they want from them. Salespeople use it to control people's minds and get them to make the decision to buy.

It is important that you understand your emotions and those of others, as it will help you read their minds. Practice listening with empathy when someone is talking to you, and ensure that you stay open and calm.

Flattery can be combined with manipulation. However, the combination of flattery and manipulation is very powerful and works well at controlling and influencing people. The individual being manipulated may not even know they are being manipulated, making this type of manipulation harmful.

The person being manipulated may be doing everything the manipulator asked them to do out of loyalty and love, thinking that the manipulator has their best interests at heart. They do not know that the manipulator is manipulating them for their own advantage and don't have their interests at heart.

Now that you are aware of this, you will know when you are being manipulated and when to use the techniques to your advantage. Remember to use the methods we have discussed for good and not to harm anyone.

If you are in a situation where you need to understand what someone is thinking to know the right words to say to them, the techniques in this book will guide you. You have been dreaming of traveling to a particular country for a holiday, but your partner prefers another destination; you can put ideas into your partner's mind, and they will think the idea of traveling to your dream destination is actually their own idea. Also, if you are trying to get a crush to like you and you are not sure if they will say yes to your friendship offer, you can study their body language and come up with the right words.

Reverse psychology can help you in dating. You might act as if you are not interested in having a relationship with a woman when you really like her. This will make the woman start seeing you as a very interesting person and make up her mind that she wants to be with you.

You can use the techniques we have discussed in this book in different situations. As you continue to practice the methods, you will get better and become a master at using dark psychology to understand people's thoughts in no time.

Printed in Great Britain
by Amazon